In the House *of* Muhammad Ali

The publication of this book
was enhanced by a gift
from the ECHO Foundation of
Austin, Texas, and especially through
the generosity of Adele Hay Fath.

In the House
of
Muhammad Ali

A Family Album
1805–1952

Hassan Hassan

The American University in Cairo Press

I dedicate this album to
the memory of Great-Aunt Nimet,
Princess Nimet Mouhtar,
without whom
I would never have met
the Reeds or the Robsons.

Contents

Illustrations

Introduction

by Elizabeth and Robert Fernea

Hassan Aziz Hassan is a descendant of Muhammad Ali, the ruler who a hundred and fifty years ago attempted to bring Egypt out of its Ottoman past and into the modern world. Prince Hassan is also a painter of note, whose works are found in private art collections around the world. His painterly eye for detail and for shapes and images is evident in these memoirs of his youth, which begin in his early childhood and end in 1952, when he was twenty-eight years old. Hassan was our friend when we lived in Egypt during the 1960s. His intellect and dry sense of humor enriched our lives then and he has remained our valued friend through the passing years.

Prince Hassan offers the reader a picture of the royal past in Egypt, as seen from the vantage point of an insider, a young grandnephew of King Fuad. This perspective is more or less absent from recent histories of Egypt, which tend to focus on the postrevolutionary period after 1952, the time of presidents Gamal Abd al-Nasser, Anwar Sadat, and Hosni Mubarak. Not surprisingly, most accounts of the last years of the monarchy in Egypt tend to dismiss its royalty as wastrels and debauchers. Hassan implicitly takes exception to this view of his family. He argues that the 150 years of Muhammad Ali's dynastic rule were crucial for the economic and political development of Egypt, which led to its present nationhood. This is the time when France and Great Britain jockeyed for position in Egypt, then regarded as the crossroads to Asia and Africa. As Sir Richard Burton wrote in 1853, "Egypt is the most tempting prize which the East holds out to the ambition of Europe, not excepting even the Golden Horn." For the Suez Canal provided access to the profitable trade routes to these lands. Muhammad Ali's descendants struggled to maintain the nation's independence in the face of growing western intrusion and control.

Prince Aziz, Hassan's father, was the nephew of King Fuad I. He was a founder and supporter of the early Wafd Party, the objective of which was to seek an end to colonialism and usher in an independent nation-state. For this reason, the British, then de facto rulers of Egypt, exiled Aziz to Europe. Hassan's great-aunt gave her jewels to help found Cairo University, again against the policies of the British, who did not want to open higher education to Egyptians other than their selected élites. In these and other ways, Hassan stresses that many in his family strongly identified with Egypt and contributed to the movement for independence.

But these points are only a small part of this work, a few threads of the complex tapestry of the past, which Prince Hassan has woven for readers and illustrated with previously unpublished photos from family collections. Here, described with charm and humor, are the houses and palaces and gardens, the state occasions, the royal parties, the jewels and the gowns which he remembers from his childhood. Here also are the everyday activities of a group of people who were socialized from early childhood for rule and responsibility. Of course, not all members of the royal family accepted their responsibilities, but many did, giving generously of their time and wealth to Egyptians less fortunate than themselves. This is the side of the story which the author clearly feels has been neglected in most other histories, whether willfully or through lack of knowledge. In constructing this chronicle, Hassan has been able to draw not only on his own memories, but also on the stories told to him by other members of his family. As a result, this work is the text of an oral history, as well as a collection of personal memories, about a crucial period in the formation of modern Egypt.

Prince Hassan recalls other aspects of his childhood memories with less pleasure. For while he celebrates his ancestors, he is not uncritical of them. And while he records pleasures in Egypt and in travels abroad, there are also memories of the loneliness and isolation of a young boy whose schooling and guardianship were a matter of royal counsel rather than the decisions of his own parents. After the death of his father, Prince Aziz, Hassan and his siblings were sent to and removed abruptly from schools in Egypt and abroad. Hassan himself studied in Turkey and England and was returned to Egypt at the outset of the Second World War. At eighteen, he moved out of the royal palaces to establish his own residence and live a life of his own. This youthful past is often recalled with a certain irony, but it is not a history of complaints and grievances.

Indeed, the dignified acceptance of the changing world in this brief royal history has been characteristic of Prince Hassan's life. When many of the other members of his family went into exile with King Farouk after the 1952 revolution, Hassan remained in Egypt, his home, and has rarely left his country even for brief trips abroad. His life since 1952 has not been easy, for a royal past understandably was a cause for suspicion on the part of the revolutionary government and the confiscation of royal possessions has resulted in a very modest standard of living. Yet Hassan has earned the respect of Egyptian acquaintances in all walks of life as well as many foreigners in Cairo who have come to know him. He is a well-regarded member of the Egyptian artistic community and his good taste and unfailing good manners have won him the respect of some of the most stalwart critics of the old royalty.

Prince Hassan has had a long time to think about the past recalled in this memoir and has exercised his strong sense of propriety in making the choices that structure this personal chronicle. Sensational events, personal tragedies, love and losses are not to be found in the pages that follow. Rather, the reader will be given glimpses of a world long since disappeared, a world viewed through the prism of Hassan's own memory. In written descriptions and in period photographs, Prince Hassan has created a unique family album of the Muhammad Ali Dynasty, a personal account of an important period in Egypt's long history.

Preface

Many years ago Professor Elizabeth Warnock Fernea (BJ to her friends), the well-known author and expert on Middle Eastern affairs, was looking through some of my family photographs and found them sufficiently interesting to want to publish them. I readily agreed, but she then suggested that a text should go with them. Having no imagination, I thought of putting down our modest family life, with some description of houses and habits. But an authoritative voice insisted I should add some historical notes to liven the background, which I proceeded to do.

After that, the thing lay fallow for many years, but was always present in BJ's active mind. Thanks to her, it reached the American University in Cairo Press, where it was kindly accepted for publication.

This book represents a small section of our numerous family. But it is with great sorrow that I was not able to put down my mother's family tree. I hope my Spanish relatives will forgive this omission, but all my mother's papers and the family tree have been mislaid. Now that she is no longer with us, my thoughts are often with her side of the family—the Magallons.

Prologue

The First World War was the cause of my father's exile from Egypt and his meeting my mother in Spain. An ardent nationalist, he was obliged by the British authorities, then occupying the country, to choose a foreign land as his home. He decided on Spain, a neutral country, where he was followed by quite a few other Egyptians who were also considered undesirable, among them the 'Prince of Poets,' Ahmed Shawqi. There he fell in love with my mother, a beautiful Spanish girl with black hair, big reddish-brown eyes, and a splendid complexion. She was endowed with a wonderfully easy-going disposition, and could be equally delighted with the most trivial or the most beautiful things that life would offer her. To marry my father, Prince Aziz, she became a Muslim, choosing to be known henceforth by the name of Ikbal.

My mother told me that my father had had some reservations about her changing her faith and, as a last resort, he had asked for a Catholic priest to dissuade her from doing so. The gentleman turned out to be a congenial person who spent a couple of hours sipping sherry and chatting with my father about many international matters, and finally left without having accomplished anything. But at least legal morality had been observed.

It is completely within Islamic tradition for a Muslim to marry a woman outside his faith (but not vice versa) as long as she belongs to 'the People of the Book,' that is to say the Scriptures. There are innumerable examples of this, but of course the most illustrious case is the Prophet himself, who married Miriam, a comely Egyptian Christian. Despite the considerable difference in my parents' ages, I believe that theirs was a truly carefree and happy union. It was a time when security and bourgeois contentment were something which everyone had a right to aspire to. My father was to provide my mother with all these advantages while relieving her of most of the responsibilities, with the result that she was to sail through all the upheavals of life certain that, in the end, she would get her own way by a sort of personal, divine right—and usually she did. Their two eldest children, my brother Ismail and my sister Hadidja, were born in Madrid (in 1918 and 1919 respectively), followed by my sister Aicha in Shubra in Cairo (1921), and myself in San Remo, Italy (1924).

My father chose to build in San Remo as a place of political security, as he explains in a letter to Wasif Pasha (at the time Bey) Ghali,[1] and, as things turned out, it was to remain our most permanent home. But of the two places—Shubra and San Remo—Shubra was by far the more important because of its historical past. It had been the favorite palace of Muhammad Ali the Great, the founder of our dynasty. As history crops up every now and again in these family reminiscences, it is only fitting to briefly outline some of Muhammad Ali's life and origins, for without him nothing that follows would have ever occurred.

---

[1] The letter was in the possession of Ambassador Ibrahim Ghali.

Chapter One

Muhammad Ali
1769–1849

Passions, theories, reasons all pop up like Jacks-in-a-Box as soon as some-one steps out of a teeming crowd to make his own way in life and, even-tually, if powerful enough, to condition the lives of others too. When it is on a scale that upsets the already dealt hand of the superpowers, one can imagine the commotion that it can create—in Muhammad Ali's case, with a chain reaction that makes it almost impossible today to open a book on the international history of the period without coming across his name. For it was he who would reanimate a country that was at the hub of the ambitions of Britain, France, Russia, and Turkey, with all the ramifica-tions extending to Austria and Prussia—that is to say, the great powers of the day. The United States was still a distant land which had not yet solved the economic differences between its northern and southern states; Spain continued to indulge in its splendid and romantic isolationism, its eyes riv-eted far away in the western hemisphere; and Italy was on the way to re-establishing its national unity. The Arab world lay dormant within the fold of the Ottoman empire.

It was an empire that had passed its zenith, but was held together by the swords of a soldier race and generations of remarkably able foreign min-isters who played off the country's foes without apparently their ever sensing it—a rearguard action pitting wit against superior modern tech-nology and weapons. In its capital, in a setting of incomparable beauty spreading over both Asia and Europe, reigned the Sultan-Caliph, tempo-ral sovereign and high pontiff of Islam. The Imperial Majesty was sur-rounded by a court of the greatest dignity and decorum, of the most sen-sitive refinement, love of the arts and of nature, but which was not incompatible with meting out indiscriminately the harshest cruelties on the monarch or his immediate male family, and on subjects equally used to giving up their lives for their country or running the risks of self-aggrandisement.

It was into this world of political agitation but not as yet of social unrest that Muhammad Ali was born in 1769 at Cavalla, a small port on the Aegean, which today is in Greece but which at the time was part of the Turkish empire, as was Egypt, where his destiny was to be fulfilled. His parents had settled there, one does not know exactly why except that the governor of the place was a relative of theirs. They lived in a roomy, whitewashed, timbered house of a style typical of the district, in fact of the Balkans and Turkey in general. It can still be visited, thanks to the Greek government's upkeep and care. It is a place of great charm, surrounded by trees and greenery, and close by it stands a handsome, if severe, equestrian statue of Muhammad Ali.[1] He was always to remain deeply attached to the place of his birth, a ravishing spot in its own right, and in later years endowed it with schools, hospitals, and other charitable institutions.

There is a theory among some that makes Muhammad Ali a Turk of quite ancient lineage. This was unheard of during my childhood and I prefer to stick to the tradition that he is of Albanian descent—a theory that is backed up by his own words in 1829 to the French travelers Messieurs de Caldavènes and de Breuvéry: "Alexander and Ptolemy were Macedonians and I too am from Macedonia." And the fact that he spoke Albanian is most significant. However, the Turkish theory is not to be completely discarded and, if correct, takes the family back another five hundred years into central Turkey. What we do know is that his father's name was Ibrahim Agha, the son of Osman Agha, who was the son of another Ibrahim Agha.

Muhammad Ali was a handsome, energetic young man obsessed with the importance of physical fitness, always challenging his young friends to dangerous feats or trials of endurance. On his father's early death, the Governor of Cavalla, noticing his aptitude as a leader, gave him the military rank of Buluk-Bashi and a company of men to help him run the unruly district, and in a series of daring escapades he soon had everything

---

[1] It should have been unveiled by King Fuad, but his death prevented this, and the 1939 war caused another delay. It was finally inaugurated by Prince Amr Ibrahim in 1949.

under control. Some time after this, in 1787, the governor arranged a match for him with a rich young heiress, Emina of Nosratli, who was also the governor's relative. Simultaneously Muhammad Ali tried his hand quite successfully at commerce.

When Napoleon invaded Egypt (1798–1801), the Turkish government required of the Governor of Cavalla a regiment of three hundred men. He provided a group of Albanians (again!), which he put under the leadership of his son, Ali Agha, and Muhammad Ali was sent as second-in-command. Ali Agha was soon to return to Cavalla, leaving to Muhammad Ali the command of the Albanians in Egypt. Having distinguished himself in some military encounters, Muhammad Ali was quickly promoted to the rank of general, Saré Chésmé, in 1801, and in almost no time he became one of the leading figures of the country, which was in a state bordering on chaos.

Although officially a Turkish governor was living in the Citadel of Cairo, Egypt was in reality in the hands of the Mamluks at this time. The Mamluks were the descendants of bought military slaves who had overthrown their masters in 1250. Among the earlier ones, there had been some outstanding military figures and rulers, but after the Turkish conquest of Egypt in 1517 they divided up the country into different strongholds or fiefs, changing from a military oligarchy into a feudal aristocracy whose members were continuously at war among themselves. They ran roughshod over everything and everyone, their name becoming synonymous with sheer terror. (Their system of violence and extortion finally kept the population of the country down to about two and a half million inhabitants.) The Mamluks were Muslims or converts to Islam, but of foreign origin. They are usually divided into two groups, the Turkish and the Circassian; the latter had the reputation of being the fiercer of the two.

In 1805, the Sultan of Turkey, fearing Muhammad Ali's rising power, tried to lure him away by naming him Pasha of Jedda, but this aroused immediate opposition in the Egyptian capital. For while the French had been hard at work supporting one faction of the Mamluks and the British another, Muhammad Ali had been the only one to take into consideration and pay attention to the native Egyptian, who was already grateful to him for keeping law and order in the capital.

Edouard Gouin, a contemporary of Muhammad Ali's, referring to the chaotic situation between 1802 and 1805, writes: "A striking contrast to the helpless situation and disorder is Muhammad Ali's austere prestige due to his comportment, scrupulously following the precepts of the Quran, a constant and familiar visitor to the sheikhs and the ulama; and also the moderate and discreet behavior of his Albanian troops, whom he knows how to keep in proper order."[1] The fact that Muhammad Ali was a sincerely devout man was also probably a link with the people of a land whose laws and ways of living were regulated by religion—whether Pharaonic, Christian, or Muslim.

So when Muhammad Ali's intended departure was announced, the Grand Council of Egypt under the presidency of Omar Makram took the decision to ask him to stay. But Muhammad Ali was not yet strong enough to brave the Sultan's wishes and in any case he wanted some legal status, something he was always to be most careful about throughout his life. So he sold some town property that he had and made his arrangements to leave. The Council then proceeded to the Citadel and asked the Turkish governor, Khurshid Pasha, to relinquish his post. Khurshid refused, saying that he took his orders from the Sultan of Turkey and not from a bunch of Egyptian peasants.

By then about forty thousand people had assembled at the foot of the Citadel to see the outcome of the Grand Council's decision. When they heard that it had been rejected by the governor, the crowd started a siege of the Citadel, some climbing up into the highest minaret of Cairo, that of Sultan Hassan, and firing on the garrison from there. Then the ulama stepped in with a proclamation asking the rest of the population to rise against Khurshid and in favor of Muhammad Ali. Opposed by such overwhelming odds, the governor had to give in, but not, to do him justice, before he had received orders from Istanbul to do so. The Sultan in Turkey, to retain some semblance of authority over Egypt, was obliged to bow to the will of the people and the power of his vassal: the Imperial Assent was dispatched by messenger as well as the usual honors and trappings that went with it.

Muhammad Ali then finally agreed to receive the reins of government from the hands of the Grand Council in a public ceremony at which all the powers and representatives of the land were present, and at which the mili-

---

[1] Edouard Gouin, *L'Egypte au XIXe siècle, histoire militaire et politique, anecdotique et pittoresque de Méhémet-Ali, Ibrahim-Pacha, Soliman-Pacha (Colonel Sèves).* Paris: P. Boizard, 1847.

tary swore allegiance to him. This is perhaps a unique example of an oriental ruler being plebiscited and acclaimed by his country in his own time. Muhammad Ali's prestige was enhanced by a military success often glossed over, but of primary importance, for it completely changed the country's historical evolution. In 1807, the British, under the command of General Mackenzie Fraser, landed in Alexandria and tried to take Egypt with the help of the Elfi Bey faction of the Mamluks (Elfi Bey was already dead). While Muhammad Ali was busy in the south fighting the Mamluks, a series of inconclusive skirmishes and battles were taking place in the Delta. On March 29, the British had occupied the town of Rosetta, but were routed by a Turkish and Albanian force and obliged to flee to Alexandria, leaving behind them 120 captives and the heads of ninety of their fallen comrades, which were subsequently sent to Cairo.

Muhammad Ali, arranging a hurried truce with the Mamluks of the south, returned to Cairo and from there sent on his troop, to win a crushing victory at al-Hamed, near Rosetta, on April 21. The British retreated to Alexandria, leaving a considerable number of casualties and prisoners. The heads of the fallen were exhibited on pykes throughout Cairo (the people had to see with their own eyes), but the prisoners, in contrast with the first batch from Rosetta, were well treated.[1] "Muhammad Ali by his sensitive generosity wanted to redeem the chilling cruelties of the soldiery, the brutal pleasures of the population. All the care that the wounded needed was administered to them. He did not refuse one of their requests or petitions. Majors Moore and Wagesland and twenty-two other officers were given comfortable lodgings in the Citadel."[2] Finally, after an exchange of prisoners had been arranged, the British left the country on September 19 and Muhammad Ali entered Alexandria on the 20th.

But the Mamluks, unrepentant, were still plotting against him. It was literally a duel to the death for power. Having failed with the British, they rose up in arms again three years later, in 1810, this time on their own. On July 28, they were beaten by Muhammad Ali in person at that most violent battle of the Bridge of al-Lahun. After this defeat he tried to win

---

[1] Henry Herbert Dodwell, *The Founder of Modern Egypt.* Cambridge, Eng.: Cambridge University Press, 1931.

[2] Gouin, *L'Egypte.*

them over to a pacific coexistence by bestowing on them important or lucrative positions and gifts, but to no avail: another conspiracy was unearthed in 1811 to kill Muhammad Ali, his family, and the principal members of his government. After long hesitation about how to deal with these insatiable conspirators, Muhammad Ali decided to strike a decisive blow. He lured them to the Citadel, where, caught in an unmaneuverable situation, all that were there were massacred.

Throughout the country the remaining Mamluks were hunted down and, if caught, executed. It was the Night of Saint Bartholemew, the Sicilian Vespers, Peter the Great eliminating the Strelitz. Their terrible and violent end is very much in the tradition of the medieval history of Egypt. (Indeed, Muhammad Ali may have been inspired by the example of Saladin's massacre of the forty thousand men of the Fatimid guard, with their women and children to boot.) The European world was appalled; the Romantics had been fascinated by these brilliant and colorful warlords, and the politicians, which is more important, had lost their favorite clients in the country; they suddenly found themselves empty-handed, the pack of cards had slipped between their fingers. But for Egypt it was the end of a nightmare, the end of feudalism and civil strife. However grim, one must regard this date, 1811, as marking the country's first steps into the modern world and the end of a medieval night.

This was the last of the Mamluks, apart from a small band that fled south to the Sudan with their families and treasures, leaving behind them a trail of death and desolation. Except for their unquestionable physical and military valor, and the beauty of their tomb-mosques, there is almost nothing kindly to be said in their favor.[1]

Muhammad Ali now had a relatively free hand to do as he wished—relatively, because plots and counterplots against him were always rife, both outside and inside the country. The way was paved with continuous strain,

---

[1] After such an upheaval one may wonder what happened to those of their women and children who did not leave. Most of the orphaned male children were brought up for military careers, quite a few in Muhammad Ali's own household. As for the remaining families, one hundred thousand feddans were set aside for their welfare and upkeep, many of the ladies being looked after and protected by Muhammad Ali's wife, Emina of Nosratli. Anwar Abdel Malek, *La Formation de l'idéologie dans la renaissance nationale de l'Egypte, 1805–1892.* Paris: Sérifloc, 1969.

unending vigilance, treachery, and disillusions. But despite these handicaps, he started on an amazing career, reforming everything, and especially the army, with the technical advice of foreign experts. With more modern military methods he was to conquer the Sudan, Wahhabite Arabia, Palestine, Lebanon, and Syria. In two other campaigns he smashed the might of the Ottoman empire, thanks to the inspired leadership of his son Ibrahim Pasha, thus winning autonomy and hereditary possession of Egypt. But of Ibrahim Pasha more anon.

Muhammad Ali was convinced of the necessity of modern technology. While firmly upholding religion and respecting its customs, he turned his back on the East in other matters and sent delegations of Egyptians to Europe to learn the arts and sciences of the day. Beautifully engraved portraits were made of this band of young men who were to be the nucleus of modern Egypt. Although the collection has now been dispersed in Egypt, it can still be seen, complete, in France.

On the land itself, canals and waterways were drained and repaired and dams built, the one in the Delta allowing the region to have three crops a year instead of one; arable land was increased by 30 percent and cotton introduced into the country. Now that the waters in the Delta were under control, the peasants no longer had to fear years of drought. This new-found security was to bring to an end a most ancient custom, the offering of public prayers for a high Nile flood, which had finally become an official ceremony. It was a fine, if rare, manifestation of human solidarity (or was it fear?) when religious antagonism was set aside and "the khatib who presided over the Friday sermon of the Great Mosque (that of Amr), Said Omar Makram, leader of the Sherifs, the ulama and students, the Arab and Turkish Imams, were all mixed together with the rabbis, the Coptic, the Greek, and the Armenian Patriarchs, the Latin priests from the Holy Land, the Italian missionaries of propaganda, the Marronite priests, all praying together."[1] On this occasion, August 16, 1808, their prayers were answered: the Nile dutifully rose next day to the desired level.[2]

---

[1] Gouin, *L'Egypte.*

[2] On Friday, February 22, 1985, special prayers for rain, 'al-Istiksa,' were again said all over the land. A few days later it poured over Cairo and other parts of the country!

Apart from the venerable University of the Azhar and its dependencies, modern schools, virtually unknown, were now promoted. The medical school and hospital of Qasr al-Aini was founded in 1827. Industries to make Egypt self-sufficient got started successfully. The first newspaper, *Waqaya Misriya*, appeared in 1828. To finance all these enterprises in a bankrupt and devastated land, Muhammad Ali inaugurated a strong policy of commerce, which he initially supervised himself.

To ensure the waters of the Nile, to find recruits for the army, and in the hope of discovering gold, Muhammad Ali conquered the Sudan in a bloody campaign in which he lost one of his sons in dreadful circumstances; the ensuing vengeance was equally merciless. Khartoum was founded in 1823. The last Mamluks who had fled there, many of them living on rafts on the Nile, were dispersed.

It was Muhammad Ali who for the first time since the Arab conquest of Egypt allowed church bells to be rung in public. His attitude to the different religious minorities was perhaps the most important of the sociological events that were to allow the consolidation of national unity. The first title of Bey to be conferred on a Christian was under Muhammad Ali, and the first Christian Pasha was Nubar, under his grandson Ismail.[1] Titles of nobility to Israelites were to follow almost simultaneously.

This enlightened attitude was to encourage many precious elements in the Near East to settle down in Egypt, where they were to contribute actively to the renaissance of the country. In its time, such a policy was an extraordinary innovation which provoked at moments opposition both from the astonished masses and from certain reactionary leaders brought up in a purely traditional manner, who were to become his political opponents. Others commented more favorably: "His indomitable and enlightened will power," writes Captain Beaufort d'Hautpoul, "has brought down the barriers that until then had seemed insurmountable between Muslims and Christians." And I think it can be said that this policy was maintained unwaveringly by his dynasty.

Muhammad Ali was a man of intuitive genius. He was illiterate and only learned to write at the age of forty; but it is not without some justifiable pride that one remembers that he was born in the same year as Napoleon

---

[1] Jacques Tagher, *Coptes et musulmans*. Cairo, 1952.

and in the country of Alexander the Great. He was of medium height, with a pleasant face and handsome, regular features that were soon to be framed by a brown beard and mustache. His eyes were blue, often with a smiling gaze which seemed to indicate that nothing escaped his notice or sense of humor. His manners were mild and courteous and his conversation brilliant and colorful. He dressed discreetly and disliked all signs of ostentation, having no use for jewelry except for a long gold watch-chain studded with turquoises.

With old age he became stouter and his beard white, his expression more fiery and impassioned, as if he could see beyond everyday events. Yet not even when his faculties were declining did he ever lose a certain majesty and dignity which imposed on all. Even his son Ibrahim, who had collaborated with him so intimately, retained to the end a feeling of awe in his presence. His last public appearance was in December 1847, when, although in very poor health and great pain, he summoned all the personalities of the land to a great banquet, at which in a long and moving speech he bade farewell to them and the country. Many of the people present were in tears. It was the end of a fantastic adventure in which quite a few among them had followed for almost half a century the young soldier from Cavalla through toil and war, disappointments and victories.

Henceforth he was to retire to private life, exhausted by his extraordinarily active career. His favorite retreat from cares of state, as I have said earlier on, was his Palace of Shubra, where Lord Byron depicts him in these lines:

In marble pav'd pavilion where a spring
Of living water from the center rose,
Whose bubbling did a genial freshness fling,
And soft voluptuous couches breathed repose,
Ali reclined, a man of war and woes.

11

Shubra
and
San Remo

The Palace of Shubra is situated on the northern outskirts of Cairo. The palace consisted originally of a large park reaching down to the Nile, carefully planted in extremely diverse sections: some were formal gardens, others were fruit groves of mangoes, guavas, and citrus trees. Muhammad Ali took an almost childlike delight in seeing orange trees in fruit and could not bear to have them picked; only the ones that fell to the ground were collected. In my childhood the place had been abandoned for many years and some of the lands sold and set back to agricultural use. The park was running wild, all the different elements intermingling in a romantic and informal manner. I remember the eucalyptus trees swaying in the wind, the mango trees with their thick, handsome foliage motionless at noon—big sacred beetles moving clumsily in their shade—and the elegance and scent of pine trees silhouetted against a striped evening sky.

The main building, the *haremlik*, was demolished well before my birth (I was born on February 22, 1924). This building had been Aunt Aziza's share of my grandparents' property. She had had it demolished when it was rumored that the British were thinking of taking it over. She felt it would be wrong to have the British use Muhammad Ali's palace for military purposes and the occupation of the country. It had been an early-nineteenth-century European's idea of Arab style, built in white marble, with loggia and balcony adorned with metal and stucco arabesques. As the palace was reputed to have been of great splendor in decoration and furnishing, fortunes are said to have been made in town from the materials salvaged when it was demolished, including paintings that were framed in the walls.

What is known as the Palace of Shubra now is a pleasance, its main feature being a vast square pool with a marble island in its center. Fountains

13

play on it, and the pitter-patter of water on stone, or the steadier rhythm of running streams finishing in the pool, is the only sound that breaks the silence and calm of the place. Surrounding the pool is a cloister-like colonnade broken up by four advancing terraces, all in white marble, exquisitely sculptured in a neoclassical, almost Pompeian style, the work of the French architect B. Coste.

The building and colonnades are enclosed on the garden side by a wall composed mainly of amber-colored windows and four doorways opposite the advancing terraces. In the four corners of the colonnade, on semicircular platforms, stand marble lions spouting water into the pool. The ceilings of the cloister are painted with decorative motifs, among which there is a portrait of Muhammad Ali set in a medallion and, in the opposite ceiling across the water, a corresponding one of his son Ibrahim.

The rooms of the building are grouped in its four corners. On the right when entering the colonnade is a drawing room with an exceptionally beautiful parquet floor inlaid with intricate designs made of rosewood. It is surmounted by a heavily sculptured ceiling painted dark blue and gold with a handsome chandelier hanging from its center. The room is furnished with nineteenth-century armchairs and chairs in the style of Louis XV lined up against the walls. Two ornate consoles, topped by high mirrors, are to be found on the left as one enters, and on the opposite wall another console completes the furniture of the room. On the darkly paneled wall between the two consoles should hang a full-length portrait of Muhammad Ali. The remaining three walls are almost exclusively composed of windows with striped carnation-red and silver-gray curtains. Bronze wall brackets give additional light, their crystal festoons intermingling with the floor-length draperies of the curtains.

Two other suites in the corners of the building were used as bedrooms, all walls and ceilings gaily painted with oriental arabesques. In the fourth corner is the billiard room. The wall on the right when coming in is decorated in the Italian manner of the period, depicting a romantic landscape with classical ruins, almost a *trompe-l'oeil*, but the flowing architectural lines that frame it are very Turkish. The three remaining walls are almost all windows, with, on the whole length of the facing wall, a deep divan.

Originally this had been the dining room, but when King Louis-Philippe of France (1830–48) sent Muhammad Ali the billiard set, with its superbly sculptured bronze-handled cues, he housed it there. This was one of the many presents exchanged by these two rulers of such different worlds but who seemed to have been staunch friends.[1] For in 1848, Muhammad Ali, during a Mediterranean cruise, had landed at Naples where news reached him that Louis-Philippe had been obliged to abdicate; it is said that this shock provoked the first signs of senility in Muhammad Ali; boarding his ship, he sent orders for the rest of the fleet to follow with his troops, and he set out to rescue his friend.

The fleet did not move, as his son, Ibrahim Pasha, with a regency council was already governing the country. But the anxious son, on hearing of his father's strange behavior, took ship and gently brought the old man back home, where soon after, on August 2, 1849, he died in Alexandria, dispirited and broken-hearted at what he considered his failure to bring, or to have shaken, Egypt further into the modern world. He is buried in the Citadel of Cairo in the Alabaster Mosque[2] that he built and that gracefully dominates the city with its slender minarets and Ottoman cupolas. Below them squadrons of white pigeons wheel in ever-changing formation, while lonely kites rest motionless in the air on outstretched wings.

By the time of Muhammad Ali's death his name had become a legend. Certainly among the common people his prestige must have been immense, for the Consul-General of Great Britain, in a letter to Lord Palmerston, writes: "All over the Turkish empire one could hear people say, 'If God would allow me, I would give ten years of my life to add to those of our old Pasha.'" Also in present-day Egypt, tribute is again being paid to him as 'the founder of modern Egypt,' and public acknowledgment was made to him when on the new twenty-pound note of 1976 there appeared an engraving of his mosque on the Citadel with the inscription, 'Mosque of Muhammad Ali the Great at the Citadel.'

Muhammad Ali's well-loved Shubra had changed considerably when

---

[1] Although there is no acknowledgment of the donor, only the name of the engineer who was in charge of the transfer from Egypt, the obelisk at the Place de la Concorde in Paris is a gift of Muhammad Ali to France. Another obelisk sent at the same time to London acknowledges the donor's name.

[2] Ibrahim Pasha had wanted it of marble, but Muhammad Ali had insisted on alabaster to stimulate a waning local industry. In 1983, the whole complex of the Citadel was restored, and the domes of the mosque were covered with a shiny silver metal, which is incredibly ugly and spoiled Cairo's principal landmark.

we were there in the early 1920s. We lived in two perfectly simple modern villas that my father had built in his share of the grounds. (The only words embossed on my parents' stationery were 'Shubra Village.') I have no memory of the furniture, but I suppose it must have been the same that we had when we moved to town. This was heavily sculptured dark Chinese, monumental and uncomfortable. But there was another set I was particularly fond of which dated back to Muhammad Ali: some of the consoles and a very beautiful round central table made of porphyry, with cornflower-blue, enameled bronze bands encircling the pieces. From one or two old photographs, I see there was also quite a lot of furniture in hybrid 'Arab style' and, as always with my father, an enormous collection of arms on big, red-felt-covered panoplies.

The dining room was again in hideous arabesque adapted to European forms—a merger that should have never occurred. It had two large sideboards with mirrors in the middle; these were surrounded by shelves which, to my childish eyes, seemed to go upward almost to the ceilings but which, of course, did not, as the ceilings at Shubra were very high.

The second house was the *salamlik*, where, for the most part, my father entertained political guests. On the ground floor were spacious reception rooms with armchairs and couches, usually stacked against the walls, a study for my father's business activities, and this time a much more sensible dining room in a fine, polished dark wood. The floor above was given over completely to a vast library and a few guest rooms.

It was perhaps in this house that the Wafd party came to life, as Prince Omar Toussoun, my father's brother-in-law and cousin, had been the one to suggest to Saad Zaghloul Pasha the founding of this political party that at its origins was to have the unamimous backing of all the people, in all the different strata of society. My father, among many others, was to help finance it, and Shubra was to become one of its active rallying points.

A third house was the servants' quarters and the main kitchens, where reigned two head cooks and their underlings. (My mother said to me, 'In my father's house we ate very well, in your father's house we ate supremely well!") There were of course also some outbuildings for the laundry, the garages, and other utilities.

The three buildings were grouped together in a perhaps not impeccable garden; in its farthest corners, it was very 'countryish,' but formal around the living quarters. It was an amusing place for us children, where we could be driven around in a horse-drawn carriage on sand-covered paths or play with some old cannons and other armaments too big to enter the house.

Our part of Shubra al-Balad (Shubra Village), as the district is called, was the farthest away from the city and still very much part of the countryside. In the farthest sections of the garden—those adjoining the fields—and also down on the water's edge, there lurked wolves, foxes, and jackals which at times would be hunted down. At night some would roam near the houses, and the foxes, strange to say, were the ones that attacked the nightwatchmen, who in the morning would exhibit their torn garments.

On and over the Nile there was a delightful, two-storied wooden chalet, a sort of tea pavilion, which afforded a beautiful vantage point for sunsets. But my father also used it to sleep in when coming back late at night, his chauffeur valeting him so as not to wake up the household. It was built in a style which had details reminiscent of nineteenth-century Medieval, simplified and not at all fussy, the whole construction appearing like a fragile cube painted a reddish, rusty, color. On each side of it antique cannons pointed outward over the Nile. But we would go to the nymphaeum, or *fisqiya*, as the marble quadrangle with its fountains and pool is called in Arabic, to play about in, rowing on its water or lingering by its colonnades in an atmosphere of peace and tranquility.

In later years my aunts would give receptions in the nymphaeum for passing royalty, or huge charity balls, when the building would come to life for a brief moment, only to relapse again into its deathlike silence. Aunt Aziza, who was fond of the place, would go there regularly once a week to have tea with a few friends.

Aunt Iffet lived in another part of the garden in a most charming little house built on the top of what looked like a step-pyramid. The house had been elevated in this unusual manner so as to have a view of the Nile. But it turned out that, as the building was facing west, the afternoon sun was too hot to bear comfortably and a screen of eucalyptus trees was planted between it and the river, but in a manner which still allowed one to see the glimmer of water and passing sails. The platforms leading up to the house were planted with flowers, shrubs, and eucalyptus and pine trees. Stone stairs flanked by white marble urns overflowing with flowers communicated from the ground to the main door of the house facing the river, while identical stairs at the back façade led down to the grounds.

The central hall was of alabaster, with a little sunken fountain surmounted by a white dome ribbed with gold. In this room Princess Iffet would give small parties, each guest seated in front of a round silver tray for dinner, while around the fountain her Circassian or Turkish maids danced their national dances in their lovely native costumes. Often each tray would be arranged with different porcelain and glass so that the guest had an individual color scheme to suit his or her personality. In the evenings or afternoons when Aunt Iffet was not entertaining, one would sit on rocking chairs on the platforms surrounding the house while a flute player, hidden among the trees, played my aunt's favorite instrument.

Princess Iffet (1876–1962) was the great beauty of her day, and when she sailed on the royal yacht, the *Mahroussa*, to save Turkish refugees from Thrace, dressed in her severe nurse's uniform, she was often likened to a rescuing angel. She was a most energetic and generous person, with both her time and her money. President of many charitable organizations, she was untiring for the welfare of others and would never refuse personal assistance to individuals or causes even when it was a strain on her own finances.

She also had a very soft spot in her heart for animals and, when in Istanbul, if ever she found any being led to market she would buy them up—flocks of sheep, geese, or goats and chickens, anything that came her way—and have them set free within the hillside grounds of her home. Not all the animals were grateful, and her grandniece Aziza Sabet, who was living with her, tells me that some of them, especially the turkeys, would attack innocent passersby. Aziza and her brother Fayd proceeded to turn this into a game and they would see who could get through from one end of the garden to the other without being molested.

But there were no such goings-on at Shubra, where everything was under careful management, whether gardens or cultivated fields. In Egypt the land is so precious that every inch of the countryside is an industry; pleasure gardens are quite foreign to most of the population, most of whom are of thrifty peasant stock. When references are made to gardens, they are usually to a grove of fruit trees.

At Aunt Iffet's death in Turkey in 1962, newspapers, radio, and other government media announced her passing away with great kindness, and her funeral was imposing. She was a person well versed in history, and during the Second World War, when traveling overland from Egypt to Istanbul, where one of her homes was a most beautiful old yali in French empire style on the Bosphorus, she would stop at all places of interest and lecture to her kalfas in Turkish. The kalfas were female servants ranging from a simple maid to a housekeeper or person of confidence; they always spoke Turkish, even if they were not of Turkish origin.

The men servants were Egyptians, Nubians, and Sudanese, with a sprinkling of Turks or Albanians, and sometimes a few Italians or Armenians, these last usually working in the garages; all spoke their own languages, but here Arabic was the common denominator among them. These multinational households got on well together—people not yet being influenced by political causes that cynically exploit color, race, or religion to divide and misrule the world. Even social barriers in those days seem to have been less self-conscious.

The younger kalfas were strictly brought up, well-mannered, reliable, and virtuous, with the result that many government officials who wished to marry would inquire in a princely household if there was not a young lady available. Careful investigations of the suitor's background and character were undertaken, and if he was considered reliable and the girl willing, the wedding was arranged. The bride would be given a dowry, jewels, and furniture for her home. The trousseau would often actually start when she entered the household. Apart from her pay, she would be given in the first year a simple gold pin, in the following year something more important, and soon she had reached the stage of rose diamonds. Some of the old kalfas who did not leave had some really fine bits of jewelry, of a style highly prized in our days but which at the time was considered good enough only for household servants. The married kalfa would continue to call on her ex-mistress and maintain close ties with her previous home, on whose protection she could always depend, something that the husband had to take into consideration and that sometimes gave the wife a status superior to his own. Some of these ladies were to attain high rank through their husbands' careers.

A dear old relative, Sherifa Hanem Effendi Kurhan,[1] who died in 1974, managed to keep up the spirit of this tradition in her own way almost up to our present day—despite adverse circumstances. She had a building set up in the grounds of her house at Zeitoun, where anyone who had been

---

[1] Daughter of Princess Emina Halim and Sherif Pasha.

19

part of her household for more than five years had the right to a flat when leaving her service. If it was to get married, she would furnish it completely except for the bridal bed which, according to local custom or superstition, the bride had to provide for herself. Of course 'Aunt' Sherifa[1] would see to the wedding festivities that followed, the garden lit up with multicolored lights.

With the leveling of ways of life, these customs became an anachronism and were to fall quite naturally apart, for they also placed an impossible burden on a budget that had usually been drastically reduced through the years. This form of existence is abhorred by sociologists and politicians alike, who condemn it as being 'paternalistic'—as if the word were an unpleasant one. I have yet to meet a countryman of mine who considers himself inferior because he is poor. Being deeply religious, he knows that before God he is the equal of anyone and that alms-giving is a part of religion and a duty; thus the person who is helped does not feel a loss of dignity or under personal obligation to the donor, who is merely accomplishing his religious duty. One could go on elaborating the matter and say that therefore it provokes ingratitude. I think it may well do so, but that is perhaps just as well, since charity ought to be anonymous and not a sort of business transaction between one's conscience and those in need.

However, all this in Egypt is mitigated by the very nature of its people (I am referring to the poor), who are so dignified and courteous that their reaction in some mysterious way always seems to surpass anything that the affluent can offer. My father certainly kept up the traditions of the past in looking after the people of his household, but his wider interests for the workers and the masses were also manifested by pamphlets and newspaper articles—sometimes clairvoyant and in any case well in advance of his times.

I shall quote from something published by him in San Remo in 1924 in French, although obviously an Arabic version must have existed as it was intended for Egypt.

"Le prolétariat existe, ce sont nos frères en misères. Au lieu de chercher

---

[1] All older generations were referred to as Aunts and Uncles, even when not technically so; this gave great unity to the family, who never differentiated between close or distant relatives.

à les enchaîner, aidons les à vivre comme des êtres humains civilisés . . . .
Aujourd'hui la législation dans notre pays, Dieu merci, est entre les mains
de la nation, c'est à elle de donner des lois. Soyons généreux envers notre
prolétariat, reconnaissons lui ses droits." And to me the most moving passage is: "Il faudrait insister tout particulièrement pour que les enfants des
pauvres ou des indigents, puissent se développer physiquement et morale-
ment comme ceux des riches."

Then follow some rather harsh words: "Il est désagréable à dire, jamais
les classes capitalistes n'ont pensé améliorer par un acte généreux le sort
de l'ouvrier . . . ." And he continues: "Le jour n'est pas loin où le Capital
aussi sera contraint pour la bonne marche des affaires d'associer la main
d'œuvre intellectuelle et manuelle à l'exploitation de différentes entre-
prises."[1]

I am most grateful to a good friend for having given me this little pam-
phlet, which is entitled *La Question sociale, quelques réflexions adressées
à mes compatriotes*, as all my father's books, writings, and papers have
been dispersed except for a few letters to political friends who have seen
fit to preserve them.

When my father decided to build in San Remo, it was still the unspoiled,
flower-laden country town so well described by Upton Sinclair in *Between
Two Worlds*. The title of the book suited the place at the time we were there,
for although it was already known to a fashionable few, the 'Jazz Age' had
not yet set in, the age of cloche hats, short dresses, fast torpedoes, and rush-

---

[1] The above passages may be roughly translated as follows: "The working class
exists—our brothers in the grip of poverty. Instead of trying to shackle them, help
them to live like civilized human beings . . . Today, our country's legislation, thank
God, is in the hands of the state—it is up to the state to pass laws. Be generous
toward the working class, recognize their rights. . . . We must particularly see to it
that the children of the poor or destitute are able develop, physically and morally,
like those of the rich. . . . I am sorry to say that the capitalist classes have never
considered improving the lot of the worker by an act of generosity. . . . The day will
soon come when the Capital will also be obliged, for the sake of the smooth
running of affairs, to join the hand of the intellectual and of the manual worker in
the running of various enterprises."

ing about the Riviera or the Côte d'Azur from one party to another or from casino to casino. But I had glimpses of this period later on, as when, I remember, my mother received an elegant package from Paris. The contents were wrapped in layers and layers of tissue paper, out of which came a brightly beaded, knee-length, yellow dress. My mother held it up and made some comment about having doubts that she would ever wear it. But she was young and beautiful—only twenty-eight when my father died— and was to a certain extent prepared to join in the fun of the period. She even meddled briefly in local politics when my elder brother, Ismail, was introduced into some Fascist organization for the young. A great reception was given, at which the Italian and Egyptian flags hung side by side. There was a splendid banquet, and a representative of the Duce came up to San Remo from Rome for the occasion. I wonder now what had been in the back of my mother's mind, or who had influenced her to do such a thing; and, for that matter, what did Cairo think of it all? Unsolved mysteries of the past! San Remo, which had started as a place of refuge from the ups-and-downs of political vicissitude, finally simply became our summer home. A happy home, a home of the best of childhood memories.

The trip from Cairo to Italy was quite an expedition, as each child had his or her nurse, not to mention the maids, berberine servants, chauffeurs, and the dogs—one year our two Alsatians had a litter of seven, so there were nine of them plus two Pekinese. My father built our house, the 'Villa Reserva,' just outside San Remo toward the French border. While the work was going on, our parents rented a big villa which had been built for the Emperor of Austria and which was closer to town. Our house overlooked the sea, the main Riviera road running behind it, between us and the hills. The garden was a long, not very wide, strip of land well above the coastline. It was enclosed on the road side by a high wall and, on the seafront, by a low parapet overhanging much farther down a strip of farmland which we used to cross to reach the pebbly beach and the sea.

All rooms were facing the horizon, the ones on the ground floor opening up on a covered terrace of red-and-white marble with a fountain in the middle. The two sides of the terrace were enclosed by walls made of round pieces of multicolored glass which would catch the sunlight and spatter red, gold, and green on the marble flooring. The garden continued on the same level where the terrace ended, aglow with all the shrubs and flowers that the region offers one.

It was in this house that my father kept some of his collections, and all the odds and ends that one accumulates through life, such as some fine Arab lamps, which fascinated me, and, what I disliked most, two huge cloisonné vases the height of a man—useful, I suppose, to fill in empty corners in big rooms.

It was holiday time for us children and life was completely informal, swimming in the sea or picnicking in the hills high up among the vineyards and chestnut trees. During a heat wave we were sent to stay a whole month in a farm far from anywhere, with just beside it a mountain torrent running down a steep rocky valley filled with boulders. Farther down the sharply sloping hillside vineyards and cultivated fields were rich with summer crops, and a profusion of wild creepers overlapped everything. The rough road stopped at that level, and to reach the farmhouse one had to climb up an unruly, tough little path. When my mother would come to see us, the farmers would spot the car down below and put refreshments to cool in a well in front of the house and in a matter of minutes they were icy cold.

But most of the time back home we were at the beach playing with the children of the farmer whose land lay just below us. At night I remember running out into the garden to watch and try to catch the fireflies so luminous in the gentle Mediterranean air. From invisible plants heavy scents would assail one unaware in the darkness; everything was different then than in the daytime—another world, of mystery, but still warm and secure.

It was at this time in my life that I had two dreams that made a strong impression on me. The first occurred only once when I must have been at the most six years old, but I remember it quite clearly, as if I had actually lived the experience. The second one was to recur three times in the ensuing years in absolutely identical form, the last time when I was fourteen.

In the first dream it was a fine summer morning and my brother and sisters, with some friends of our age, were swimming in the sea fairly close to the shore, and I was sitting alone in a rowing boat nearby. Suddenly a strong feeling came over me that if I wanted to I could walk on the water around me. I got up and, stepping out of the little rowing boat, I started walking on the calm sea. It was not that the waters had solidified; it was the utter conviction in me which seemed to carry my body and make it almost weightless. Amazed, I called out to the others, "Look, look, I am walking on the water," but they paid no attention except for my elder sister, who faced me in a fury and with blazing eyes shouted, "Don't look at him; he's just showing off." At that, everybody took notice and started chiding and jeering at me, but without any really bad feelings. I took a few more steps, but, unnerved and surprised by their reaction to this phenomenon, my body resumed its natural density and I floundered into the clear, green sea.

The second dream was more sinister, although here I was to be only a spectator. It was late afternoon, the sky was overcast, with threatening, dark-gray clouds low over land and sea, covering everything, even the horizon, and in our garden there was not a glimmer of light or color. My sisters and my brother and lastly my mother were on bicycles, on a gravel path next to the parapet overlooking the sea, cycling toward the eastern end of the garden. I was watching them and calling out: "Don't go in that direction; there is a big hole over there and you will fall into it." But they were like figures in a surrealist landscape, intent on their doom, incapable of listening, riding on their bicycles toward a dark pit into which they fell one after the other while I looked on helpless to prevent them. It was a horrible sensation, like watching one's whole family going to execution.

When the subconscious is so vividly felt it becomes part of the memories of a period, just as, more realistically, the scent of peaches and carnations can still bring on for me a euphoria like a narcotic; the peculiar sulphurous smell of a white insecticide sprayed over cultivated fields, carried by men in a container a bit like a bagpipe, spells summertime by the sea; and plumbagoes and hydrangeas remain unique in my thoughts to our garden at San Remo.

The first imprint on memory marked me for a long while. Some years ago, when political circumstances would not allow me to leave the country for a considerable length of time, I felt at one point such a violent nostalgia for my childhood environment that for a few months I broke completely away from my usual abstract paintings and produced an orgy of wildflower landscapes reminiscent to me of those early days.

Our parents were very close to each other, and my mother told me that my father could not bear to be separated from her for long. Even in political matters he would ask her advice, and often her intuitive common sense would prove more to the point than the hair-splitting discussions of professional intellectuals. At times when they had had enough of a place they would get into their car and just drive away in any direction they fancied. In later years we too would benefit from these moods, and I have the vaguest of memories (or is it from hearsay?) of crossing the Pyrenees, of losing our way in a heavy mountain mist, and of skidding in a wet Madrid square, the car slowly revolving on itself.

Crossing the border at Ventimiglia I remember quite well; the scent of carnations coming from a nearby field; the sea hazy and shimmering beneath a scorching midday sun, and a young man singing and strumming his guitar for the people waiting in their cars, a carnation by his ear. One year we went straight to Melun to settle Ismail at school there, while we rented a house near the forest of Fontainebleau so as to be close to him. There were frequent expeditions to Paris, where Fakhri Pasha was our ambassador and our link with the family and Egypt.

This happy-go-lucky existence was to last only during my father's lifetime and a few years more while my mother was left in charge of us. For unexpected powers were to disrupt our quiet little world.

From being an active, slim young man, my father had become greatly overweight and was to die at the age of fifty-two from the aftereffects of an extremely strenuous slimming diet carried out under expert, but apparently still deficient, medical care. He was born at Shubra[1] in 1873, while his father, Field-Marshal Prince Hassan Pasha, as he was styled, son of the Khedive Ismail, was commanding our troops in the Sudan, which at the time belonged to Egypt. His mother, the Princess Hadidja, a daughter of Muhammad Ali the Younger, sent a dispatch to her husband announcing the birth of his first male child and smudged the inky fingerprints of the infant on the letter.

About my father's parents I know surprisingly little. My grandfather had an active military and governmental career, but was to die very young (1854–88). He was known for his extraordinary kindness, very good looks, and the same sort of absolute integrity of character that distinguished his favorite brother, the Sultan Hussein. He was the nominal commander-in-chief of our army in the unsuccessful Abyssinian campaign,

---

[1] I stick to what my mother told me of my father's birth; according to the rest of the family, he was born in the Palace of Gezira, as were all his brothers and sisters. Collections of documents such as the Abdeen archives, which would have contained this information, were not within my reach.

but it being his first military assignment at the age of nineteen, the actual command was left to a group of more experienced generals. One of these, Rashid Rakeb Pasha, was to save my grandfather's life at the battle of Karakur, which was to make his descendants, the Shafiq Pashas, very close to our family. During the Russo–Turkish War of 1872 he led the Egyptian contingent, which distinguished itself, but he insisted on bringing back his men to Egypt during the winter months, as they would have been unable to stand the bitter Asian climate. His early death, before his father, the Khedive Ismail, was to deprive his children, according to the law of the time, of the inheritance of their grandfather the Khedive, and make us one of the poorer branches of the family.

As to my grandmother, photographs and portraits corroborate her beauty, but one of her chief attractions was her gaiety and wit. Great-Aunt Nimet told me that when the young girls of the family went out for drives they would all try and get into my grandmother's carriage, where it was sure to be most fun. Her father had been brought up in Turkey during the unpleasant reign of Abbas I in Egypt and had become the inseparable friend of Prince, and later Sultan, Mehmet Rashad. Perhaps because of this association, on her marriage to my grandfather the Sultan sent her as a wedding gift an emerald necklace reputed, according to a Turkish imperial source, to be the finest in quality in the world—something, I should have thought, that would be difficult or impossible to assess or assert. Still, there was a life-size portrait of her wearing this piece of jewelry, which was composed of one single row of large, round, flat stones that was impressive.[1]

My grandmother must have suffered terribly at her husband's early death, since they were devoted to each other. Rumor had it, and it may well have been true, that he had been poisoned while in Turkey by the Khedive Ismail's enemies, and for the rest of her days she was to tremble for the lives of her children. She never remarried and in old age became more and more of a recluse, earning for herself the reputation of being an eccentric; of course, kind souls went so far as to conclude that she was mad, which was nonsense. Any form of individualism in the East is

---

[1] This portrait had belonged to Princess Aziza, but King Fuad had requested it for the Gallery of Princes at Abdeen, where it was hung. It has now disappeared.

pounced upon and malignantly elaborated, as no one can bear the idea that someone should be different from themselves. From what I gather, she was a strong individualist whom sensitivity, pride, and sorrow kept aloof from the rest of the world, although she must also have been very busy bringing up four sons and an equal number of daughters.

Like many ladies of the family, my grandmother was very authoritarian and insisted upon the strictest discipline around her, as much for the boys as for the girls. There was no pampering anyone; pride was considered the most unforgivable of sins, it being strictly reserved for one's elders; humility was something to be distilled or drummed into the young until it frequently became plain humiliation, verging at times on sadism. Whatever shortcomings this kind of education may have had, and short-comings it most certainly did have emotionally, when later on it came to be abandoned by some people, everything went to pieces. It was heavy medicine but apparently a necessary one.

My father was given a thoroughly military education, finishing his mil-itary schooling in Germany like his father before him. Coming back to Egypt in 1893, he found our army sadly reduced after the Urabi revolt of 1882, which was followed by the British occupation. Not finding any pos-sibilities of an active career, he decided to offer his services to the imper-ial Ottoman army. (This reduction of the Egyptian army was to result in our not having enough reinforcements to send to the Sudan in 1885 dur-ing the Mahdi rebellion, and the British stepping in to 'help,' which was the beginning of the dual control of what was to be known henceforth as the Anglo-Egyptian Sudan.[1])

Our relationship with Turkey seems to have been one of complete ambi-guity. Here was Egypt occupied by the British but nominally still a vassal of the Sublime Porte, although regionally independent. Egypt and Turkey, as we have seen, had often been in open conflict. But when peace was restored everything became officially perfectly friendly. For the struggle between the two countries had been an internal affair of the Near East and, as such, there always remained links that allowed scope for reconciliation and understanding. When the representatives of foreign powers came to

---

[1] Sherif Pasha, the senior and most respected statesman of the period, refused to sign the document of this transfer of power to the British.

congratulate Muhammad Ali after a victory over a Turkish army, the Pasha of Egypt had answered moodily: "Turks have beaten Turks." Turkey being the suzerain of the region, he had used the work "Turk" as a symbol of Eastern homogeneity, not as a racial denominator, which it could not have been in view of the complex populations of the Turkish empire.

So when my father did not find it possible to have an active military career in British-occupied Egypt, the natural solution for him was to offer his services to Turkey, the only great independent country of the Near East. But as an Egyptian he preferred to decline the pay due to an officer. He remained in Turkey until 1913 as commander-in-chief of the Turkish cavalry, which is well remembered for its brilliant rearguard action after the disastrous battle of Kirkilise in that same year.

The imperial sun was setting over Turkey. The pageantry and beauty were still there: marble palaces and white mosques bordered or dominated one of the most prestigious waterways in the world, while gilded boats glided swiftly along its shores. But the empire was breaking apart, and from the inside political unrest and intrigue were manifesting themselves in all spheres, including the army. My father was not one to participate in such activities, and he preferred to relinquish his command in 1913.

There followed the 1914 war, which was to leave Turkey shorn of its empire and the enemy in its midst training the guns of their battleships on the imperial palace of Dolmabahçe, where resided the Sultan, incommunicado. My father, to reach the Sultan, zigzagged through the enemy fleet in a motorboat that he handled himself and, landing on the palace pier, was introduced from there into the presence of the beleaguered monarch. He was never to return to Turkey, but he seems to have made quite an impression on some of his contemporaries, for not so long ago a retired Turkish officer who had known him called on my sister Aicha in Istanbul and said: "Madam, this is not a visit, but a pilgrimage."

In Egypt he should be remembered as a dedicated Nationalist and, as already noted, for his wholehearted support of the Wafd under the leadership of Saad Zaghloul Pasha, who was struggling for the independence of the country. Apart from allowing Shubra to be used for political meetings, he wrote many articles in the press and was in general as active as he could be for the cause. His efforts did not pass unnoticed at the time. In 1922, the British High Commissioner, Lord Allenby, sent him into exile for the second time (he was allowed a week's grace to settle his affairs).[1] A tumultuous crowd of demonstrators accompanied him to his train, which they obliged to stop at Shubra, all the time chanting slogans in his honor. One of these slogans could be translated as, "It is hard that you should have to abandon us, O Aziz"; and another, "Go forth, our beloved ('Azizan'), O Aziz." According to Professor Muhammad Mahdi Allam of the Academy of the Arabic Language, who took part in many of the demonstrations, the crowds were set upon by British troops swinging heavy metal chains.

When not on active service of any kind, my father would burn up energy in sports or physical activity. Yachting was one of his favorite pastimes, and he sailed many a different craft to victory. He founded the Alexandria Yacht Club, which was not then in its present location. One summer during a festival in Alexandria at which different floats were paraded, he won the first prize by presenting a float completely covered in violets, which had been brought from abroad. Riding through the peaceful countryside was not stimulating enough for his Russian-roulette search for excitement, and he was known to gallop his black stallion 'Sheitan' on the railway lines just in front of the Alexandria–Cairo train, or canter up the steep, rocky stairs of the 'Bektashi' Monastery—with an already broken arm in a sling—and have the steps watered for the descent. As the frontiers were plagued by hashish smugglers, he equipped a group of horsemen who accompanied him when he went to harass these marauders. If a particularly good fight was foreseen, friends and relatives were invited to join in the fun.

Any challenge seems to have tempted his restless nature, and he spent much time and money trying to convert desert lands into fruit groves, successfully in the long run, but he himself was not to benefit from this venture because of his early death. His name still awakens an echo in the minds of some; he is known to students of politics, but in general his patriotic efforts remain unacknowledged by time. His patriotism was based not on hatred of others but on love of his country, and at his death there was both official and popular acknowledgment of this. His funeral in a way symbolized much that had been part of his life.

---

[1] The High Commissioner informed the Palace, and the King, as head of the family, notified my father.

Sixteen days of official national mourning were ordained, two days more than the protocol for princes of the blood. A big tent was set up at Cairo's railway station square, where the royal family awaited the coffin. It arrived punctually from Shubra at 3 p.m., covered by the Egyptian green flag with its white crescent and three stars, and placed on a gun carriage drawn by six horses. Preceding the coffin was a detachment of mounted police and a detachment of lancers on horseback; a section of artillery with their men; the Eleventh Battalion of Egyptian Infantry with guns reversed; the Ninth Battalion, with drums covered in black, playing Chopin's Funeral March (a standard proceeding up to 1952); the Ninth and Sixth Infantry Battalions; a group of 200 officers up to the rank of colonel from the army and the royal bodyguard; and three naval officers in full uniform. Following the coffin were the princes of the royal family, with the Grand Chamberlain, Said Zulficar Pasha, representing King Fuad; Ahmed Ziwar Pasha, the Prime Minister, with all his cabinet; previous prime ministers; ministers of state; and undersecretaries of state. Also included were the Diplomatic Corps, the Consular Corps, high officials, the Governor of Cairo, top army officers, and the ulama.

The cortège slowly wound its way through the city to the royal mosque of Rifai, where prayers were said before the burial itself at his unfinished tomb near Imam al-Shafei. But what impressed observers most was not so much the pomp and pageantry, as the enormous, respectful crowds along the way, who, with millenary Egyptian reverence for the dead and great dignity, offered a murmured prayer as the coffin went by. They were separated from the procession by a cordon of policemen under the command of the strikingly handsome Russell Pasha on his white horse, wearing like all Egyptian civil servants a red fez, or tarboosh.

We had bidden farewell to our father at Shubra, all of us too young to attend a public ceremony. Although he had expressed in his will his desire that there be no official ceremony and that only his wife and children should attend his funeral, his wishes were not observed. Nothing would ever be the same again; henceforth paternal guidance would come to us from more distant sources.

My mother, in my father's name, gave the yacht the *Cavalla* as a gift to the nation, which was to use it as a training ship for naval cadets until the Second World War, when it was sunk bringing supplies to Tobruk. My father's affairs had been grossly mismanaged during his exiles and, just as things were straightening out he died, leaving his widow in what for her was still a foreign land, with four very young children, a confused situation, and not too friendly in-laws.

After a few more years my mother reluctantly left Shubra, being advised to take a more convenient and easier-to-run flat in town, where she managed as well as she could with lawyers, tutors, and relatives—not all of whom were hostile, but many of whom were. One refuge was left—San Remo—and as time went by we stayed there more and more, in idyllic bliss, until the disadvantages of established customs loomed up between us and a normal family life.

Chapter Three

Marg

My father had four sisters, of whom the youngest was Princess Ziba. She emanated a gentle quietude which was like a screen between one and the exterior world. A dim sort of luminosity seemed to surround her, as if she lived in a gray, limbo world of her own—also conveyed perhaps by the fact that she had very poor and limited eyesight. I felt quite drawn to her but never got to know her well. To judge by appearances, she did not have the active kindness of Aunt Aziza, or the beauty and mind of Aunt Iffet, or the wit and personality of Aunt Behidja. She was always discreet in her bearing and apparel, although this at times could be relieved by a cascade of diamonds, which gave one the impression that all worldly awareness of rank had not deserted her. Many years after her death I came across two or three people, foreigners, who had known her well and who had retained quite an impressive image of her. One of them in fact, a diplomat, named his daughter after her.

As a young girl she had a pleasant figure, lovely coloring, like all her sisters, and a face with a weak-looking chin. Silky fair hair and gray eyes added to her color charm. She was married off to a Turkish gentleman, with whom she was to lead, for the rest of her days, a pious and dignified life divided between Istanbul, Egypt, and Europe. Most of her time was spent in prayer and in the company of holy men, who guided her thoughts, and indeed at times her dreams, for she was often blessed with visions of the Prophet and other exalted persons of religion. Her psychic capacities, perhaps sharpened by this ascetic life, were not to be underestimated, as once when travelling in Sweden she manifested extraordinary sensitivity to her surroundings. When shown up to her hotel room in the company of her lady-in-waiting, she stepped out on the balcony, only to recoil in horror, saying,"Who is that poor girl lying crushed on the ground?";

whereupon she proceeded to give a detailed description of an unfortunate person who, only a few days before, had committed suicide by jumping from that very same place.

Her existence could have been considered passably normal, and we suppose happy, if there had not been a major setback (or had it been a deliberate omission?): she was childless. Somewhere in the family—I know it wasn't her, she was terrified at the thought—the idea got started that she would be a more suitable person to bring up Prince Aziz's children than their mother, who, as a foreigner, could hardly be expected to know much of the family's ways. The idea took root and blossomed forth into a grand family council, composed of my aunts, Great-Aunt Nimet (Grandfather's sister), her husband Mahmud Mouhtar Pasha, and our great-uncle (Grandfather's brother), King Fuad, who had been invested by my father with the supreme authority over our upbringing.

The discussion for our abduction was well underway, and everything pointed to our landing in Aunt Ziba's reluctant lap when the unexpected occurred. King Fuad had had time to think over the matter, and plans for our future were shaping in his head, making him prefer that we should be brought up by his sister, Great-Aunt Nimet. Unexpectedly again, Mahmud Mouhtar Pasha joined his wishes to the King's, saying that all their children had grown up and that their house was empty without them. Great-Aunt Nimet readily accepted, being utterly devoted to her husband and always willing to accede to his wishes. So Aunt Ziba escaped this turbulent intrusion into her life and returned to her solitary five-prayers-a-day at Bebek in Istanbul, and we were to join Mahmud Mouhtar Pasha and Great-Aunt Nimet at Marg, their estate near Cairo.

For years afterward I was to deeply resent our having been wrenched away from my mother. It was only much later on, at a very mature age when the harsh realities of life were finally beginning to pile up around me like tombstones for my illusions, that I was able to understand our relatives' reasons for subordinating sentimentality to the observance of certain conventions. All this was strictly against my father's wishes, since in his remarkable will he had stated that we should be brought up away from the rest of the family, and that my brother and myself should become an engineer or a doctor and my sisters qualified medical nurses. He also specified that we should not touch a piaster of our inheritance before the four of us were successfully earning our livings by means of the stated professions, for the day would come when this would be the only means we had for our livelihood. But there was no one to heed the words of the dead, and the living—with perfectly valid reasons of their own—were to steer us in a diametrically opposite direction.

The first to leave our mother's side was Ismail, followed after a few months by my sisters, and after another interval myself, being at the time eight years old. I remember well arriving with my mother at Marg on a beautiful afternoon and meeting Great-Aunt Nimet for the first time. She was seated at the end of the main drawing room by a window which gave on the gardens, wearing a pale-blue gown reaching to the ground with a large cluster of diamonds on her chest in the shape of a bow. She was very composed, very regal, hair carefully set, extremely expressive dark eyes and a firm, wide mouth. On a chair to the left of the couch on which she was seated, a little bit apart and on her own, a lady was discreetly keeping her company, one of those silent witnesses without face or voice always to be found around more important personalities.

I was terribly shy, hardly managing an answer when spoken to, but fortunately quickly fascinated by a most beautiful painting hanging behind my aunt. It was a Claude Lorrain landscape, whose calm and serene atmosphere I grew to love dearly, and which somehow has managed to remain my favorite mood painting for life. My mother appeared to be her usual self, talking about me, my habits and health. All seemed very normal until the moment for parting arrived, and then she could no longer restrain her tears. I did not completely realize what was happening, that I was leaving her forever, and although rather bewildered it was not till later that I was to understand the full magnitude of our loss. Now I was looking forward to meeting my sisters, whom I had not seen for months. Ismail had already left for Robert College in Istanbul.

Looking back, I find it surprising how easily I adapted myself to my new life despite the fact that I was passionately attached to my mother. But for her it was the handing over of her last child, her youngest one, and the solitude of a future with an empty home. Once a week she would come to see us and we would have lunch together; and, finally, Marg was only twenty minutes away from Cairo by car, but somehow as time went by it seemed to be worlds apart.

Princess Nimetallah, Great-Aunt Nimet, was the last surviving daughter of the Khedive Ismail and as such the last of King Fuad's sisters. This

35

gave her a unique position in the family, and both her royal brother and other relatives often accepted her opinion on many subjects as law. Her exceptional personality enforced her privileged position. Of a naturally regal appearance without any affectations or mannerisms, a sure sense of humor which would lighten up her dark eyes, eyes that could also be most forbidding, an education combining old traditions of the East and the West which are finally remarkably similar, abreast with the latest philosophical, scientific, or literary thought in several European languages, she was a devoted wife and an impeccable public figure. To make these rather formidable qualities more palatable, she had that most precious and elusive of gifts—charm and magnetism.

She was born to rule, as a despot it must be said, and however much I may have disagreed and found myself in conflict with many of her uncompromising decisions, she invariably left me with the uncomfortable feeling that she was in the right. After many years, and having seen many surprising things, she still remains the most commanding figure I have as yet encountered, and my feelings for her of respect and admiration remain unabated.

Her husband, Mahmud Mouhtar Pasha, was a Turkish *grand seigneur*, a soldier and diplomat, and an authority on the interpretation of the Quran whose works have been translated into several languages. With all the tact that springs from true kindness, he made it a point to make us always feel cared for, as if of his own flesh and blood. He was to die from a heart attack on a trip to Europe, and I think my great-aunt never really recovered from the shock; she became sterner and the atmosphere at Marg more austere. From then onward her health began to waver and fatefully decline; diabetes had set in.

When Great-Aunt Nimet decided to live at Marg, the Palace of Marg was a simple hunting lodge set in grounds that were part desert and part marshes. In front of the house, which was on slightly raised ground, was a row of six date trees growing out of the sand. From this wilderness my great-aunt was to create a home of great charm. The marshes for miles around were drained and the desert pushed back, beautiful formal gardens laid out around the house, lawns and a small forest of eucalyptus trees planted. The same tall, rustling trees bordered long alleyways, while clipped hedges enclosed groves of fruit trees. Tennis courts and a golf course sprang up under unrelenting supervision and care.

The six date trees in front of the house remained, but beyond them on a lower terrace a rose garden stretched out, with— as its central ornament— a life-size red-granite statue of a seated female pharaonic figure, its face heavily mutilated, that had been found in the grounds. It was reflected in a small pool, beside which a banyan tree gave shade to a square clearing furnished with garden tables and chairs. From there a path bordered by white-trunked palm trees led to one of the main arteries of the garden,which was on still lower ground. A new wing was added to the house itself, which was solidly built with double walls of stone, separated by an empty space to isolate the interior temperature from the exterior.

A very lovely color was given to the garden by the coral-red sand that covered its paths and alleyways; these were bordered by a cactus-like plant that hugged the ground and flowered with a lilac-colored bloom called in Arabic 'the staff of life.' The more athletic bignonia, with its rubbery cluster of orange flowers, smothered a palm log-hut where I used to practice my piano; other bignonias, intermingled with purple bougainvillea,went up into dark casuarina trees, making bright garlands from tree to tree.

Fifty gardeners, under the control of an old Italian, kept this very harmonious creation in impeccable state—not a leaf out of place, not a grain of red sand in disorder, for wherever we walked a gardener would appear from nowhere, in a rather uncanny manner, to sweep away with palm branches the marks left by our footsteps. No detail was too small to escape our great-aunt's notice, and it was this careful supervision that gave the place an air of a royal residence, for the palace itself remained a roomy, unpretentious, one-storied house which Great-Aunt Nimet would refer to as her bungalow. Plans were periodically drawn up for the building of a real palace, but fortunately they were always shelved.

Uncle Ala'adin, Great-Aunt Nimet's son, lived in a two-floored modern villa in another part of the grounds, with its own enclosed garden. When I was living there, it was something of an ordeal coming back at night, for Uncle Ala'adin's Great Danes would charge at anyone without discriminating between family or strangers. The guards, who knew the dogs well, would suddenly take on a vague, absentminded air, hoping, I suppose, to see one thoroughly frightened, which I usually was, for although I have always been fond of animals I was never to get on intimate terms with this lot.

The house was furnished by a well-known European decorator in contemporary, mid-1930s, style, which I found very impersonal but which, I suppose, was considered appropriate for a young bachelor who had just finished his education in America. At Great-Aunt Nimet's at least there was a collection of fine paintings, superb rugs, and a happy mixture of furniture, arranged very personally and intelligently. Her grandson Faizy, with his devoted English governess Miss Holbeech, lived in another house, sparsely furnished in the most functional manner.

My sisters and I alternated, or were divided up, between Uncle Ala'adin's and the main house. Our day was well organized, being given over to a series of teachers and tutors for French, Turkish, Arabic, and the Quran, following the usual subjects of a school curriculum. For the Quran a sheikh would arrive all dressed up in his elegant robes and turban and reeking with the most subtle and nauseating scent. A tall, spare man, he would squat, tailor-fashion, his *sibha* beads moving between his fingers, while he patiently repeated with me one *sura* after another, I following the written verses, until I had learned thirteen of them by heart.

There was a luncheon break, followed by more classes or homework, and on certain days a little tennis and some mild gymnastic movements supervised by Miss Maud Machray. Miss Machray was a wonderful Englishwoman who had been in the family since her early youth as a companion to Princess Emina, Great-Aunt Nimet's sister, to whose memory she was utterly devoted; whenever she mentioned her, her face would seem to fade into some distant past superior to anything that the present could offer. When Miss Machray was dying many years later, she was heard to say: "At last I shall be seeing my dear Princess again." When I went to the hospital to visit her, I think in spirit she was already with her. She did not recognize me, although she was talking quite lucidly, for her gaze was already far away in another world.

After Princess Emina's death Miss Machray came to Marg and, when we arrived, was set to look after my sisters, and myself too when I was there. We communicated together in French, the international social language of Cairo; none of us was ever taught English.

Tall, straight, and vigorous, she had a plain face, great character, a charming smile, and a most melodious voice and laugh. She spoke Turkish like a Turk and knew all the intricacies and ways of our family. Great-Aunt Nimet would sometimes ask her to accompany her on visits, and with her yashmak on she was undistinguishable from any other lady of her position.

Nearly every day she would take us for a walk around the garden in the late afternoon until we reached the edge of the fields. There we would wait for the sun to set beyond the mud hamlet, or *izba,* of Marg, its gray cluster of huts surrounding the little mosque outlined against an orange and green sky. Slowly the light would change and the muezzin in a distant, musical voice would call the Faithful to prayer. Processions of peasants, with water buffalo and herds of sheep led by a donkey, would make their way home through a soft haze of dust, while birds flew low over the darkening fields.

In Marg we were truly in the heart of one of the most beautiful of Egyptian countrysides, famous for its forests of date trees which stretched for miles, sometimes broken up by cultivated fields, but more often thickly wooded with little waterways and canals meandering through its colonnades of trees. On moonlit nights big shafts of light would come down among them in an awesome, cathedral-like manner, and the whole place would become some great silent garden haunted by a distant pharaonic past, set in sculptured immobility.

The forest of Marg took its name from its most important village, a couple of miles away from us and the *izba.* The village was an urban agglomeration of some importance on the main road from Cairo to Khanka. Its railway station looked out of place and shabby, with a black iron railing separating the lines from the main road. But it was so rustic, and its gray functional architecture on an elevated platform so unpretentious, that it finally became something of a landmark.

Great-Aunt Nimet had rebuilt part of the village with two-floored buildings, which boasted shutters, and balconies of wood, and plastered walls painted in pale pastel colors. But basically the place remained one of mud houses and unpaved streets intermingling with unattractive buildings of plain brick. Just outside the village a water pump by a little canal was a meeting-place for the village women, who would gather there to scrub their pots and pans, all the while chatting gaily among themselves. Once their chores were done, they would pile everything on their heads and walk away in single file among the trees—stately, graceful figures, with a beauty of movement that is an inseparable rhythm of the Egyptian countryside.

At the other end of the village, the men, a rather rough, shabby lot, would meet at a café on the main road facing the black iron railing of the railway line. Beneath a provisional *hasira* awning, made of reeds and propped up by a couple of wooden poles, the clients would sit on straw-seated wooden chairs, sipping tea out of little glasses placed on rickety, three-legged, metal tables. Some would be smoking their water-pipes, in silence, their gaze far away but not missing a thing, their dignity unruffled by poultry pecking at the earthen floor at their feet; other groups of customers, merchants and peasants, would animatedly discuss business transactions; while, flowing in and out among the tables, the café attendant would go backward and forward from the interior to the public section of the coffee shop.

Aunt Emina, Great-Aunt Nimet's daughter, lived in a house close to the village, but to avoid having to pass through its narrow streets she built a road that, when coming from Cairo, started about half a mile before the village began. The new way, bordered by blue jacaranda trees, left the main road at right angles to plunge immediately into the palm forest and then emerge into the fields that almost completely surrounded the house, except for one part facing the village. A pink wall enclosed the garden and rose to meet the big, wooden garden gate, which was flanked on either side by two whitewashed, flat, classical pilasters. A similar gate, but bigger—the original one—gave on the village entrance. Inside the garden, a driveway—bordered unexpectedly by cedar trees with low sweeping branches—led to the house, which was built on a rise and painted the same color as the garden walls. It had been a hunting lodge of Ibrahim Pasha's, and Aunt Emina had managed to convert it into what to me was the most charming place of its kind in and around Cairo.

From a small glass vestibule, one stepped directly into the main room of Sheikh Mansour, as the house was called. On each side of the doorway two deep windows allowed a faint light to filter into the vast room. It was an elongated octagonal in shape, and on both right and left sides of this octagon illuminated showcases harbored some Far Eastern curiosities. The opposite two corners were occupied by two doorways leading, on the left, to a small passage with an entrance to the dining room, and, on the right, to Aunt Emina's private rooms. Both doorways were surmounted very theatrically, but extremely successfully because of the very high painted ceilings, by heavy gilt mirrors with sculptured trophies encasing the Egyptian coat of arms and crest.

At one end of the room was a monumental, square fireplace, made of old *kutahia* tiles surrounded by a marble border and mantelpiece. Over it hung a self-portrait of Aunt Emina, who had studied painting in Munich. She wears an evening gown and some red jewels, which were probably intended to offset the general color scheme—an aquatic scheme of pale blue and silver.

At the opposite end of the fireplace hung a fine fourteenth-century Flemish tapestry, with beneath it a large, gilt baroque couch upholstered in a neutral beige, where Aunt Emina usually sat. Beside it, forming a loose circle, were eighteenth-century European armchairs and casual tables grouped around a very big round silver tray which was used as a central table. It had a remarkably pretty elevated border with a festoon motif in high relief of draperies clasped by Egyptian crowns; this was all one saw of the tray, since the central part was covered by an embroidery of gold thread on blue velvet. Two large bookcases, probably nineteenth-century Louis XV replicas, spread across the walls opposite the entrance doorway. From the center of the ceiling hung a huge chandelier of enormous circumference with tiers and tiers of lights going upward in diminishing circles.

The floor was covered by two silk rugs separated by a parquet space. They were of a tiny discreet design, and similarly discreet colors, the kind where pale greens, beiges, and pinks seem to melt into each other, the more so because of the sheen of the silk. Between the two bookcases, facing the main entrance, a doorway gave on a small study containing slight, dark wooden furniture. A small *bureau-plat* served as Aunt Emina's writing table, which despite its feminine size had a predominant atmosphere of military discipline: a goblet holding four or five pencils all the same size and equally well sharpened, pens in a separate container, and a few personal but not cumbersome souvenirs. And always a cheerful bouquet of garden flowers. On the walls were two good academic portraits of her parents, and an elegant little Venetian Guardi in grays and blues that lightened up the room.

A doorway on the left gave access to the dining room—big and furnished in gleaming, dark Chinese–Chippendale, which set off porcelain wonderfully. The curtains were of plain red silk from China, which always shocked me, although they sound eminently appropriate. It was something in the color; they suited the furniture but not the house.

From a bay window in the study one stepped out on a terrace the same size as, and perpendicular to, the entrance lobby of the house. On summer evenings it was an extraordinarily lovely place from which to look at the view. The garden, with a lot of purple bougainvillea and herbaceous borders, sloped down toward the velvety green fields; they, in turn, stretched out to a feathery gray line of eucalyptus trees that bordered the invisible waters of the Ismailiya Canal, on which tall, pointed white sails moved leisurely, like some particularly successful mobile come to the rich countryside.

Aunt Emina was to me one of the most delightful persons of her generation. Although to some people she seemed unbending and irascible, which she may well have been at times, my relationship with her since my childhood to her last days on the Bosphorus remained without a cloud. I have memories of walking with her through the summer countryside at Kitzbühl, or in later years dining at Sheikh Mansour in the garden by candlelight. I can hear her tinkling, delightful laugh and see the expression of pleasure on her face when in congenial company or surroundings. I remember her accepting to come in semi-disguise to a fancy-dress party I gave just after the war (in 1946 or 1947), staying until midnight, enjoying herself thoroughly, and, having seen everything and everyone, departing in high good humor.

All the same her presence imposed on many, and I have seen people instinctively drop a curtsy when greeting her, and others address her by the title of Princess. When the latter occurred, she would quite firmly point out that she was the daughter of a princess and not of a prince, and therefore had no right to any such title, since the children of princesses inherited only their father's name and status. Her sense of decorum went so far that when she received from her mother, among other magnificent jewels, a most remarkable tiara, she used it for some time abroad but then had it broken up as it embarrassed her to be bedecked more ostentatiously than other members of the family who were her elders.

She entertained splendidly at Sheikh Mansour. The octagonal room would be turned over to dancing, and then, when one stepped through the study to the terrace, one would find a huge marquee divided up into different sections, dining rooms, drawing rooms, all arranged with the taste and perfectionism which were so much part of her.

Married to a Turkish diplomat, Aunt Emina was often abroad and it was Sheikh Mansour's fate to remain for long periods shut and unused. The house and the lands around it had been given to Aunt Emina by her mother at the time of her marriage, but before that it had remained unoccupied for many years. A band of robbers, thinking it an easy prey, had tried to break into it, but the garden watchmen had resisted and something of a siege had taken place. Finally a truce was called and, after a lot of palaver, it turned out that the robbers were not local peasants but men from the desert region, misfits among the agrarian population, who had turned to brigandage for lack of suitable work. On hearing this, Great-Aunt Nimet had found them jobs throughout the estates, many becoming night watchmen in her own garden, and law-abiding citizens for ever afterward.

It took hardly a few minutes to get from Sheikh Mansour to Great-Aunt Nimet's place, which was always referred to as 'Marg.' One passed through the village in a matter of seconds and straightaway into fields that stopped at the *izba*, which pressed its huts on the home farm. The place was filled with water buffalo, from whose milk was made the most incomparable yogurt I have ever tasted. Next came the ocher-colored administrative buildings of the estate, which preceded the main entrance to the garden—a simple, low, black iron gate surmounted by an arch of evergreens springing from the hedges on each side of it.

The entrance could be spotted from afar in the flat landscape by a clump of gigantic old eucalyptus trees standing like sentinels opposite it. Behind the trees, parallel to the road, passed the railway lines. The train, if desired, would stop just opposite the garden gate at a modest, wooden platform with two posts holding a board announcing the name of the little station—'Nimetallah,' my aunt's name, so baptized by King Fuad as an affectionate compliment to his favorite sister who lived there. Further down the road, adjoining the garden, was a brick factory also belonging to the estate.

The obvious question now arises as to what sort of relationships were maintained between two such different sectors of society, visibly poles apart, as the peasant population and the landlords. Naturally this was conditioned by the personalities of the people concerned, but there were everyday functional ties as well and some of a more subtle nature.

Perfectly normal and nice but absentee landlords, who might not supervise personally their given instructions, would get a bad name through their greedy stewards, who would exploit both their masters and the peasants ruthlessly; both, for different reasons, would be almost helpless in their hands. By contrast, an exemplary landowner such as Sherifa Hanem

Effendi, mentioned earlier, would spend some of her time on her estates (even her mother's tomb was there); she had built 150 houses for her peasants, a school, and a public bath which was shared by the two sexes, who used it on alternate days. Sherifa Hanem continued to receive courtesy visits from her peasants years after she had had all her lands confiscated by the republican military government that took power after 1952.

Marg was a halfway house between these two segments of society, being so close to Cairo. Uncle Ala'adin ran the farm and tried to bring in innovations in the local agriculture. The men servants who waited on us at table (white jackets and gloves, black ties, trousers, and shoes, red tarbooshes) were all local peasants who had come up 'through the ranks' into the house. But the major-domo who presided over them was one of the more important kalfas, assisted by another maid who had the dual role of being in attendance on Great-Aunt Nimet.

Great-Aunt Nimet herself would make unannounced visits to the *izba* dispensary to see if everything was running properly, ready for first aid or minor ailments. It could house eight to a maximum of ten women and the same number of men. But only minor surgery, or ophthalmological and gynecological interventions, were carried out there; more serious cases would be referred to hospitals in Cairo, some of which were family-supported institutions. The oiling of these wheels within wheels that went to make up a whole were a common religion (I am referring to a majority) and a stable government.

Strange as it may seem to people conditioned by years of propaganda, both at home and especially abroad, no one was above the law. The everyday advantages or abuses of influence, position, and wealth stopped before the law courts, and it is only fitting here to pay homage to the Egyptian magistrature of the period, which proved itself to be of complete integrity and incorruptibility. It was considered quite justly to be the nation's crowning glory without which no security exists. And the basic patterns of behavior which a common religion, never neglected by either side, imposed on both worlds was a subtle bond which kept everyone flowing in the same direction.

On official religious holidays, the Eid al-Kabir or the Kurban Bairam, one would see on the normally rustic Marg road a line of cars bringing members of the family, or dignitaries and their wives, to call on Great-Aunt Nimet or sign their names in the Visitors Book. At the garden entrance the two porters, wearing caftans with the family colors, dark-blue trimmed with cyclamen, would perform a deep *téménah*—that particularly Turkish way of bowing in which the right hand reaches toward the ground and then up to the chin and the forehead—when ushering the guests in, and announce their arrival by ringing an electric bell communicating with the house. There Béchira, an old black eunuch, a relic of harem days, dressed in a smart black frock-coat ('stambouline'), would help visitors out of their cars, aided by a few other men in dark-blue suits, all of course wearing tarbooshes on their heads. If the visitor was of princely rank, or the King in person, a double row of kalfas—usually about fourteen of them—would make a passageway in the marble paved hall, bowing to deep *téménahs* as the person passed between the two lines, which uncurled like a breaking wave.

On these occasions table covers ('sirmas') of velvet embroidered with gold thread would be brought out, only to be wrapped up again in tissue paper afterward, and put in a cloth satchel, to be stored away so that the thread would not tarnish. Refreshments would be served from fine crystal ware, Bohemian nineteenth-century colored glass, or silver goblets (rarely of gold) which had matching covers and saucers.

When the moment of departure arrived, the guest would be escorted to the house door by one of Great-Aunt Nimet's ladies, some of the kalfas would be hovering around for minor services, and discreetly in the background one could feel, if not see, other attendants ready to step in if needed. Everything was kept in a low key, as simple as possible and in a pleasant, hushed atmosphere. From time to time one could hear coming from the reception rooms a well-known laugh or recognize the voice of some equally well-known personality. In the speeding car on the way back to Cairo the visitor might emit a sigh of relief that the visit was over, but there would also be an unspoken feeling of contentment about something harmoniously done in a world without a cloud.

In the opposite direction from Cairo, toward Khanka, the untroubled countryside would remain unchanged except for some horse-drawn carts carrying whole families of peasants, dressed in bright, shiny holiday finery, singing or clapping their hands to the beat of a *darabukka* or tambourine. Pretty fellaheen children would wave to passersby or wait by the roadside in the hope of selling some dates placed in woven fiber baskets. Farther down the road, by a bridge spanning a canal, was a police checkpoint for commercial vehicles, and after that the way passed through one of the loveliest spots of the region, mainly the great forest of palm trees, but also with clearings containing groves of oranges, lemons, and tangerines.

One early summer Great-Aunt Nimet was staying with her brother, King Fuad, and his wife, Queen Nazli, at the Palace of Montaza in Alexandria, when my sisters and I were summoned to join them. There we were to meet our great-uncle and his wife, and their children, the future King Farouk and his sisters, the Princesses Fawzia, Faiza, Faika, and Fathia. King Fuad, out of veneration for his mother, whose name, Ferial, began with an 'F,' had wanted all his children's names to start with the same letter. (Her tomb is in the same chamber at Rifai as his own; but, out of respect for her, hers is the bigger and the more important of the two.)

Accompanied by Miss Machray, we boarded the train at Cairo station and got off at Sidi Gaber, one stop before the Alexandria terminus. A chamberlain and two bright-red palace cars were waiting for us, and we drove off to Montaza. On arrival there, we kissed our aunt's hand and were served with refreshments of sherbets (fruit syrup mixed with water) and fresh fruit. Then a lady-in-waiting appeared, followed by a maid (short black dress and white apron, very different from Marg kalfas) carrying on a tray presents for us from our uncle the King: a diamond brooch for Hadidja, a sapphire-and-diamond pendant for Aicha, and a child-size gold watch for me. We asked the lady-in-waiting to thank and convey our respects to His Majesty. Then we were introduced to our cousins on a large, covered marble terrace on the first floor, where we played about with a ball until Queen Nazli appeared, accompanied by Great-Aunt Nimet, who presented us to her. The Queen[1] must have had a most magnetic personality, for, forgetting my usual shyness and all thought of proper manners, I ran to her and, jumping up, flung my arms around her neck and kissed her soundly on both cheeks, much to the general merriment.

Then the Queen and Great-Aunt Nimet left, and some time later we were ushered into a small drawing room, where we were presented to the King.

---

[1] Queen Nazli was the daughter of Abd al-Rahman Sabri Pasha and the sister of Sherif Sabri Pasha.

1. Muhammad Ali Pasha

2. Muhammad Ali's birthplace at Cavalla and his statue there.

3. Muhammad Ali Pasha.

4. Muhammad Ali in a contemporary print.

5. Ibrahim Pasha,
son of Muhammad Ali.

6. Miniature of Ibrahim Pasha,
painted during his visit to Paris.

7. *Toussoun, son of Muhammad Ali.*

8. Princess Felixsun, wife of the younger Muhammad Ali, the mother of the author's grandmother.

9. The Khedive Ismail in Albanian uniform.

10. The Khedive Ismail
in Cairo.

11. The Khedive Ismail in
his last days, in Turkey.

12. *Neshedil, mother of Great-Aunt Nimet, wife of the Khedive Ismail. Neshedil, Djananiar, and Felixsun were all Circassian ladies.*

13. *Princess Djananiar Hanem Effendi, the last surviving wife of the Khedive Ismail.*

14. The author's grandfather,
Prince Hassan, son of the Khedive Ismail.

*15. Princess Hadidja, the author's grandmother, in
Oriental costume. She was the daughter of the younger
Muhammad Ali, son of Muhammad Ali the Great.*

16. *Princess Fatma, daughter of the Khedive Ismail, sister of the author's grandfather.*

17. *Egyptian postage stamp issued in 1998 commemorating Princess Fatma's donation for the foundation of Cairo University.*

18. *The author's grandfather, Prince Hassan (seated), who married Princess Hadidja. Standing, a close friend, Fahmy Pasha.*

19. The Khediva Emina, wife of
the Khedive Tewfik, daughter
of Prince Ilhamy, son of Abbas I.

20. The Khediva Emina.

21.Great-Aunt Nimet (left) and her daughter Aunt Emina Tougay, with her dog Demir, probably at Bad Kissingen in the summer of 1936.

22.Great-Aunt Nimet, followed by Aunt Emina Tougay, being received by the palace chamberlains on her return to Egypt from travel abroad.

*23.Great-Aunt Nimet
(Princess Nimetallah).*

24. Princess Chivekiar.

25. Princess Chivekiar.

26. Prince Ismail Daoud.

*27. King Fuad as a young prince, .
probably in exile in Italy.*

28. King Fuad with his son Farouk, Prince of the Said.

29. King Fuad visiting the Valley of the Kings, Luxor, Upper Egypt.

30. *King Fuad inspecting outlying villages in Egypt.*

31. *King Fuad with Prof. Pierre Lacau, the head of antiquities, in Upper Egypt.*

33. *King Fuad's cortège, coming out of Abdeen Palace at his funeral.*

32. Shamm al-Nasim in the Qubba Palace grounds. From left: Princess Ulfet Fazil, mother of Prince Abbas Halim; King Fuad; Sultana Malik (wife of Sultan Hussein); Princess Nazli Halim; Aisha Hanim Izzet, wife of Prince Muhammad Ali Hassan; Mme. Mahmoud Pasha Sabet, cousin of Queen Nazli; Princess Huriyyah Hamdi, King Fuad's sister-in-law; Princess Samiha Hussein, daughter of Sultan Hussein. Photograph by Queen Nazli.

34. *King Fuad's coffin being borne through the streets of Cairo.*

35. The Citadel of Cairo with the Muhammad Ali Mosque,
seen from the Ibn Tulun Mosque. Photograph by Hassia.

36. The courtyard of the Muhammad Ali Mosque, with, in
the center, the ablution fountain. On the left is the clock
sent by Louis Philippe of France to Muhammad Ali.

*37. The Muhammad Ali Mosque
at the Citadel of Cairo.*

38. A room in Muhammad Ali's harem quarters at the Citadel (now the military museum).

39. The nymphaeum of the Palace of Shubra (low water).

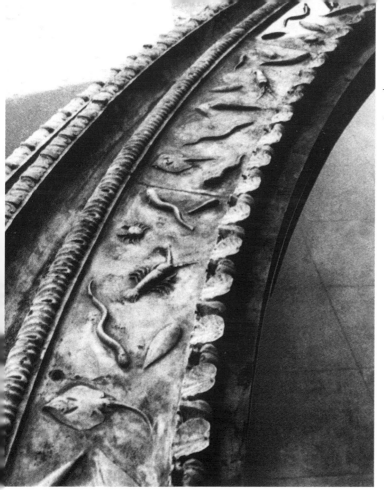

40. Sculptured detail in marble, the nymphaeum.

41. The nymphaeum of the Palace of Shubra.

42. The billiard room
at Shubra.

44. *The Egyptian army barracks of Qasr al-Nil, later taken over by the British. The northern wing on the left is the Palace of Said Pasha, near the Qasr al-Nil bridge, where the Nile Hilton stands today. Photograph by Dimitri of Greece.*

43. *Drawing room in a corner of the nymphaeum, Shubra. Courtesy Adrian Richardson.*

45. *Said Pasha's Palace on the Nile, the third wing of the Qasr al-Nil barracks.*

46. A room in the Palace of Qasr al-Nil built by Said Pasha. The electric fittings were added by the British when it was being used as an officers' mess.

47. The Khedive Ismail's private home is shown in the background. In the foreground is the home of one of the royal ladies, which communicates with the main building. The palace stood in Giza, was demolished by the British, and is now the site of the zoological gardens.

*48. Prince Hussein Kamel's Palace,
near Cairo University.
The palace has since been demolished.
Courtesy Max Karkegie.*

49. Palace of Qasr al-Dubara on the Nile.
The Citadel can be seen faintly in the background, left.

50. Left to right, Semiramis Hotel,
Palace of the Khediva Emina (Walda
Pasha), and the British Embassy on the
Nile. Collection of Adrian Richardson.

51. The author's father,
Prince Aziz Hassan,
during his military service
in Germany.

*52. The author's father
in San Remo, Italy.*

53. The author's father in Alexandria Harbor.

54. The author's father as commander-in-chief of the Turkish cavalry, with his officers.

55. The author's father and one of the first planes in Egypt. He was in charge of early aviation activities in the country.

56. *Princess Iffet Hassan,*
sister of the author's father.

57. *Princess Iffet Hassan in*
pharaonic dress, 1911.

58. *The author's mother with Aicha, Hadidja,
and Ismail at Shubra Palace.*

60. King Farouk in his garden in the Palace of Qubba.
The photograph was taken by the author's sister Hadidja.

59. The author's mother
holding Hadidja in Madrid.

61. Crown Prince Muhammad
Ali Tewfik visiting the
Muhammad Ali Mosque at
the Citadel of Cairo, 1938.

62. King Farouk, 1940s.

*63. The author as a baby
with his mother, sisters, and
brother at San Remo, Italy.*

64. *Princess Faika and the author, at Montaza Palace. Princess Faika was the third sister of King Farouk.*

65. Mrs. Rosalind Reed and the author, in London.

*66. In back, from left to right, Miss Maud Machray, the author's sister
Hadidja, Princess Fawzia (sister of King Farouk), and the author's sister
Aicha. In front, between Miss Machray and Hadidja, from left, Princess Faiza,
Faizy Mouktar, and Princess Faika. Photograph taken at the Palace of Qubba.*

68. Princess Fawzia in Cairo, 1940s.

*67. Princess Fawzia, eldest
sister of King Farouk*

69. *Princess Faiza (center) in Turkey with the the Egyptian ambassador's wife, Attia Madame Emin Fuad al-Monasterly. The ambassador is in the background.*

70. *Princess Faiza at the Egyptian Embassy in Turkey in front of a portrait of King Fuad.*

72. *Princess Faiza presenting trophies to an Italian officer at a horse show near the Pyramids, about 1950. To her right is Muhammad Taher Pasha.*

71. Princess Fawzia (center) and Princess Faiza (on the right), both wearing the uniforms of the Red Crescent Society. Just behind Princess Faiza is Hanzade Sultan.

73. Costume ball given by the author. Seated with an international group are the author (second from left in back row) and Princess Faiza (smiling in center, holding out her hand to Jojo Nahoum, son of the Grand Rabbi of Egypt).

74. Family lunch at Abdeen Palace. King Farouk seated fourth from right. On his left are Prince Izz al-Din Hassan, son of Prince Muhammad Ali Hassan; Prince Ismail, the author's brother; and the author.

75. Muhammad Ali Raouf Bülent, husband of Princess
Faiza and grandson of Princess Fatma Ismail.

76. Prince Ismail, the author's
elder brother, who volunteered
for army service during the
1948 Egypt–Israeli war.

77. The author's sisters
Hadidja (seated) and
Aicha in Uncle Ala'adin's
house at Marg.

78. Princess Aicha (middle), sister of the author, reviewing Girl Guides in the Cairo Opera House, now gone.

80. Uncle Ala'adin Mouhtar with his Great Danes at Marg.

*79. Dinner at Abdeen Palace. Right to left: Aunt Emina
Tougay (daughter of Great-Aunt Nimet); Princess Mahivech
Said Toussoun (daughter of Princess Emina Behruz Fazil);
Princess Emina Toussoun; unknown (face hidden); the
author's sister Aicha.*

82. Left to right: Seldjouk Sultan of Turkey (daughter of Princess Emina Halim and wife of Djezouli Rateb), Ülviya (daughter of Prince Abbas Ibrahim Halim and wife of Shehriar Rateb), Dji-Dji (Mrs. Djéhankir Rateb), Nimetallah (daughter of Prince Amr Ibrahim and wife of Munir Sabri, son of prime minister Hassan Sabri Pasha); in the background, wearing white tuxedo: Shehriar Rateb.

81. Aunt Emina Tougay, 1951, upon her presentation to King Farouk's new queen Nariman.

83. Alexandria, the summer of 1952, in front of Princess Faiza's house. Left to right Bob Simpson (the private secretary of US Ambassador Jefferson Caffery), Farida (a Turkish cousin of Bülent), Princess Faiza, the author, and Fayd Sabet.

84. The author, 1953.

85. Ras al-Tin Palace, Alexandria.
This is the palace from which King
Farouk left Egypt, 1952.
Photograph by Dimitri of Greece.

86. Painting of the author, Hassan Aziz Hassan, by Jean-Denis Maillart, 1946.

Here there was no question of forgetting oneself; we kissed his hand and did our *téménahs* down to the ground, stood to attention, hands clasped in front of us, and listened to his little speech: We were to work hard at our studies and obey our Great-Aunt and Miss Machray in all matters.

The King had an alarmingly severe appearance, with handlebar mustaches. He seemed to us children remote and set apart from humankind; but this was a childish impression, for he was simplicity itself in family circles, and as long as he lived we had continual proof of his concern for our welfare. We felt his presence, however distant, in all our doings, and in later years I was able to confirm this. Of all the members of our numerous family he was unquestionably the one who did his best to take over our father's responsibilities toward us.[1]

As a child King Fuad had left Egypt with his father, the Khedive Ismail, for exile in Italy and, when he grew up, went with the future king of Italy, Victor Emmanuel, to the military academy in Turin. Later, as a young man, when not busy with state duties he had led the life of an Edwardian man of fashion, in the sense that he had been very much a ladies' man. But almost overnight he had come to the throne and turned out to be a most remarkable, hardworking, and enlightened monarch; and, on his marriage to Queen Nazli, a devoted husband and family man.[2]

Like his ancestors Muhammad Ali and Ibrahim Pasha, who literally almost to their dying breath would go through the length and breadth of the land to see that projects were being carried out properly and did not remain a dead letter through indifference or corruption, King Fuad would insist on supervising many things himself and, at times, with what one might think unnecessary precautions. I have been told by a particularly discerning foreign ambassador who was in Egypt during his reign that receptions at Abdeen were extremely well thought out, even down to the smallest details of the cuisine. This was because the King often supervised everything himself. If there was an especially delicate or tricky ceremony ahead, he would have the whole thing run through the previous day in

---

[1] J. W. McPherson, in his very charming book *The Moulids of Egypt (Egyptian Saints-Days* (Cairo: N.M. Press, 1941), refers to him as "that kindhearted monarch."

[2] Before his coming to the throne, he had been married to Princess Chivekiar, by whom he had an only child, H.R.H. Princess Fawkiya; a son, Ismail, died young.

front of his unerring and attentive eye. He would not entrust to others what was an official, and therefore national, occasion which would reflect on the country as a whole. Within the family, for the same reasons, he would keep a watchful eye. If anything was seen to be amiss, quick retribution would follow in the form of a palace chamberlain with a message from the royal head of state. If things really went too far, the person in question would be officially and publicly ostracized.

King Fuad was strongly opposed to the ladies of the family frequenting the diplomatic missions. Personal acquaintances and friendships were permitted, but never of an official character. The exception was Aunt Aziza, who was asked by him to entertain once a week the wives of foreign diplomats to tea. She had a beautiful dining room in her villa at Giza, the walls lined with showcases filled with priceless jade which, with the right lighting, created a fairy-like atmosphere. She herself was a kind and simple person, but like many of her generation had the appearance of being slightly aloof, as if everyone had been assigned an allotted amount of vital space in life, with invisible barriers for privacy. She was the one of her sisters-in-law whom my mother liked best.

Largely through King Fuad's personal efforts, Egypt was in 1922 again recognized as an independent country. By royal decree in the same year a democratic constitution was drafted, based on the Belgian constitution, and the final version was promulgated—again by royal decree—in 1923. It was by this constitution that the country was to be run henceforth. According to one authority, "It left something to the future, but tried to guarantee the people an effective participation both in the administration of public affairs and in the framing of laws and their execution. This Constitution guaranteed equality before the law, individual liberty, inviolability of the domicile and property, liberty of opinion and assembly, a free press, and compulsory education for both sexes." And again: "The importance of the power conferred on the King as opposed to the parliament in the 1923 Constitution can be appraised correctly only if the prestige of the House of Muhammad Ali is brought into account. The King enjoyed admiration, even veneration, in Egypt as shown by many National Hymns."[1]

---

[1] Jacob M. Landau, *Parliaments and Parties in Egypt,* with a foreword by Bernard Lewis. Westport, CT: Hyperion Press, 1979.

King Fuad dextrously steered the ship of state through one of the most crucial and complex moments of contemporary history, filled with patriotic riots, manifestations and aspirations, and British opposition to complete self-rule. One had to know how far to go and no further without risking the loss of what the country had gained, for gunboat policy was still rampant. Thus, in 1926, when the Egyptian government formulated a wish to lighten British control over the Egyptian army, three British warships were sent to Alexandria, and no one had any trouble in taking this rather heavy-handed hint—or in remembering the bombardment of the second capital by the British fleet in 1882. Similarly, industrialization was discouraged, for the looms of the British Midlands had to have priority. But this was skillfully by-passed through the founding of a national bank with all-Egyptian capital—a measure that was to allow the great industrial center of al-Mahalla al-Kubra to emerge and to furnish the country with the necessary textiles.

One of King Fuad's lesser-known interventions, according to one of the most distinguished Islamic scholars of the time, Mrs. Devonshire, was his work to save and prevent the destruction of medieval Cairo, which was going on at an alarming rate around the Azhar University. She comments on "the enlightened taste of King Fuad, to whom archeologists owe the timely rescue of so many precious monuments. It was H.M. who prevented the destruction of the whole façade of what is perhaps the most beautiful house in Cairo, the Sehemy Palace." We are also indebted to King Fuad for founding innumerable cultural and scientific enterprises and institutions, said to number over eighty. The only share that he requested for himself, at the death of his brother Prince Ibrahim Hilmy, was the Prince's remarkable library, which was housed at Abdeen.

The King's death proved to be a turning point in the history of the country, and he was greatly mourned and regretted—to this day. After a revolutionary eclipse of many years, his imposing stature is beginning to take shape in the minds of many concerned with the history of Egypt.

King Fuad, it must be admitted, was inadvertently the cause of the mishandling of the interior decoration at Abdeen. He was informed that the Palace needed renovating, and a budget of two million pounds was set aside for the purpose. As the King had neither the time nor any interest in these matters, he was advised to give the work to what he was told was a competent European decorator, who proceeded to push into distant corridors very nice pieces of already existing furniture and replace them with contemporary replicas of period pieces. But the decorator's most ridiculous and offensive blunder is in the Byzantine Room, which he filled with art-deco reliefs. In our days these may be considered amusing or modish, but the whole arrangement is a museum piece of bad taste and a complete anachronism. A few rooms were not molested and are all right, among them the Throne Room, which is dignified and in the spirit of the country. I am afraid that Montaza did not fare better than Abdeen; only Ras al-Tin survived without damage.

But to return to that particular day when we were summoned to the Palace of Montaza. After the King's departure, we went to lunch with Queen Nazli and some of her ladies, Great-Aunt Nimet, and our cousins, all except Princess Fathia who was too young to be at table with us. In the middle of the meal the King joined us and everyone stood up. Then, in a voice like thunder, he said: "Asseyez-vous," the Queen sat down; "Asseyez-vous," Aunt Nimet sat down; "Asseyez-vous," and we all sat down!

Here is the menu of one of these family luncheons, in this case one that took place at Qubba:

> *Hors d'œuvres variés*
> *Filets de sole Orly, sauce tomate*
> *Cotelettes d'Agneau à la Villeroy*
> *Cailles au Riz*
> *Céléri à la Moelle*
> *Petits pois frais à la crême*
> *Dinde de Fayoum rôtie*
> *Pommes de terre Anna*
> *Salade pointes d'asperge*
> *Umm Ali,[1] Gateau du Soleil, Dessert*

After lunch we went for a drive with our cousins in the wonderful gardens. Montaza was a self-sufficient paradise. From afar one saw a wood-

---

[1] A delicious Egyptian dessert, served hot and a bit like bread-and-butter pudding but with almonds, raisins, and pistachios, and a lot of cream.

ed promontory stretching into the waters of the Mediterranean with—in the middle, on a slight hill—the turrets and towers of what seemed some Ruritanian castle. On coming closer, the castle turns out to be a strange construction of arches and wide balconies of stone and marble which defies definition, certainly not esthetically beautiful, but extremely pleasant for a seaside residence, and, looking back from the present day, it does have a certain harmony of its own which is quite valid.

But Montaza's crowning glory are its gardens, with beautiful sheltered coves and bays on the sea, sandy beaches, and savage cliffs and rocks. On the land side, close to the sea, are sturdy if uninteresting casuarinas; in the center part are, or I should say were, lawns, rockeries, rare flowers, and a profusion of different varieties of trees; near the main entrance one was greeted by especially splendid date groves of great height.[1] Yet it must have been a very empty paradise for our cousins, for we were the first children they had ever met, and when little Princess Fathia was taken away before lunch, she cried out after me: "I want the little boy, I want the little boy," as one might ask for some new-found toy.

So every Friday we went to spend the day with our cousins, either at Montaza or at the Qubba Palace in Cairo; but my sisters more often than myself, for I was soon to leave for school abroad. These 'Fridays' lasted as long as King Fuad lived, then they were discontinued. We were to be replaced by a group of attractive young people more in keeping with Queen Nazli's wishes.

Money. For the first time in my life I started to hear the word. We were poor, we must be careful—no extravagances, keep accounts even of our small amounts of pocket-money, for we were poor and must learn to do as best we could with the little we had. I was quite taken aback with this unexpected state of affairs. When I was fourteen I inquired what I could

---

[1] Since the government takeover in 1953, changes have taken place, apart from the building-over of parts of the garden. Here is a report of the Ministry of Agriculture, 1982: Of the botanical gardens, 40 feddans are no longer under cultivation, 5,000 trees have been felled, over and above 250 of the famous palm trees. Most of the other trees that have survived have been attacked by parasites.

hope to inherit later on, and I was told in a mournful voice: "My dear, if you'll get fifty pounds a month you'll be lucky!"

It was only when I was to come of age that the situation was to clear up and I found myself in possession, much to my surprise and relief, of a quite adequate income, nothing to do with that terrifying fifty pounds. Until then I suffered from an acute insecurity complex, being sure that starvation, or at least a life of extreme privation, was awaiting us. All this of course was part of the principle that one should browbeat and not spoil the young. My reaction to this past nightmare, when I did come into my income, was to squander my money left and right for the first three or four years until I got used to the idea that there was nothing more to fear. The thought of making money had never occurred to me, since I had not as yet met anyone with business associations. And, even now, I have to admit that people in business seem to be almost semi-mythical creatures whom I envy from afar.

The supreme council for family problems or affairs was the Majlis al-Balat (from the word 'Palat' or 'Palatium,' according to Aunt Sherifa), a council of state composed of the Crown Prince, the Sheikh al-Azhar, the Grand Mufti, the Sheikh of the Sharia tribunal, the President of the Senate, the head of the King's Privy Council, and the Public Attorney.[1] As an intermediary between this august body and ourselves we had a tutor, 'Sir' Abdel Hamid Soliman Pasha,[2] a charming gentleman with the most suave manners, an inscrutable smile on a bronze-colored face, and hands that shook slightly when holding his coffee cup or lighting his cigarette. To him we would go with requests for a bigger allowance, a new car, or extra money for traveling expenses, to which he would always agree as it was understood that we would not call on him except at our great-aunt's instigation. The idea that my brother and I should ourselves go and ask him was of course a gesture of courtesy; but the intention was also for us to get used to being in contact with practical things. The first time I went to see

---

[1] I am indebted to His Excellency Hassan Youssef Pasha for this list.

[2] Egyptian officials were allowed to accept foreign decorations when our Foreign Office saw fit. There were several among them who received British knighthoods, but of course never used the title, which would have been ludicrous for a man, let us say, like the leader Nahhas Pasha, who was a Sir Mustafa!

him on my own was when I was about sixteen. He was living in an extremely handsome mansion in Zamalek, which is now an embassy.

Great-Aunt Nimet, as our guardian, decided all general lines of conduct, such as schooling, travel, and the like. Only if there had been a crisis or important problem would the Majlis al-Balat have intervened. The only major decision for which I was personally indebted to them came when I turned twenty-one—when they decreed me fit to take possession of my inheritance. I then called on the 'Balat' (an abbreviation we always used) at Abdeen and left my card with a word of thanks. (And it was on this occasion, in this administrative backwater section of the palace, that I noticed all that nice furniture and interesting pictures that had been secluded there, as I mentioned before.)

Here I would like to dispel a myth about the wealth of our family. The glamor of the word Egypt led the world to suppose us in possession of fabulous fortunes, something like the Ptolemies in Roman times. In those days of almost complete agrarian economy, Egypt was indeed a wealthy country with a legendary past that the ancient world could hardly match. But when Muhammad Ali arrived in Egypt he found an impoverished Turkish province of about two and a half million inhabitants,[1] racked by internal feuds and a recent violent foreign invasion. Alexandria had been reduced to five thousand inhabitants, and there are descriptions of travelers arriving in Great Cairo in the midst of a mass of ruins and rubble and then finding themselves in the heart of the city.

Under Muhammad Ali and with the prosperity that followed, the population almost doubled, despite his numerous wars, and later it was to rise to twenty million (before antibiotics), which was the highest figure ever attained in the nation's history of five thousand years. Although some

---

[1] According to Emin Sami's almanac *Taqwim al-Nil*, vol. II, as well as the scientists in the French expedition, the population in 1800 stood at 2,460,200, and by 1848, at the death of Muhammad Ali, at 4,476,440. I go into some detail in this matter because of a new tendency among some foreign scholars to try to rehabilitate the last Mamluk period on the basis of all the commercial and artisanal guilds and institutions existing. They have always existed, throughout all periods, but they were an infinitesimal part of the population of the whole land, and this does not take into account a system of extortion and complete insecurity. The agrarian masses were at their lowest ebb.

industries had flourished up to the late nineteenth century, and did so again in the 1930s and onward, the country remained basically agricultural and, as such, a poor one in comparison with the highly industrialized states.

By the same token, our family's financial situation, deriving primarily from agriculture, was I am sure much more modest than that of some other well-known international fortunes, let alone those that today are based on oil. What allowed people to live in a certain style was the cheapness of the cost of living and the excellent value of our money—the Egyptian pound being worth a little more than the pound sterling after the Second World War. And people had no inhibitions about spending freely within the country, which was economically healthy.

Apart from the King, there were a dozen rich persons in the family, and the others ranged from being well-off to being downright poor and having to be helped by the more fortunate ones. There were *waqf* endowments, foundations from previous generations whose revenues were supposed to go to the needy members of the family, but from which, unfortunately, only a trickle ever reached its destination. I myself was to find out when it was already too late that I had been living all my life on about a third of what I should have been getting. Intermediaries, stewards, and a good number of the employees administrating the estates got the rest. When Prince Youssouf was warned that he was being grossly robbed by some of his administrators, he said: "I know, but I have quite enough with what I am getting."

Most people in our family lived in villas, rather than palaces, ranging from the modest to what might be called mansions. Palaces, apart from the state ones used by the King, could be counted on the fingers of one hand: Prince Youssouf Kemal's at Matariya, Prince Muhammad Ali Tewfik's at Manial–Roda and his ravishing house at Zizinia in Alexandria, and Taher Pasha's place at Zeitoun.

Chapter Four

Palaces and Houses

Prince Youssouf Kemal was a great hunter, and his hall at Matariya, as well as a drawing room on the right of the hall, were filled with his trophies. From the top of the grand staircase two giraffes looked down over the balustrade into the hall, which was furnished in comfortable leather couches where Prince Youssouf would often sit after luncheon with one or two of his gentlemen. In the drawing room there was a hippopotamus with a wide gaping mouth, and when I was a child Prince Youssouf would pick me up and pretend to put my head into it, much to my squealing delight.

His library was of the greatest importance and included certain publications that he had sponsored himself. But most important of all was his great collection of old maritime maps, which may well have been one of the finest in the world in private hands. In addition, he donated to the Islamic Museum many of the treasures that can be seen there today, including most of the Mamluk lamps. The Prince was generally considered to be the wealthiest member of the family, and this allowed him to indulge in having a complete night staff who did the cleaning of his house between three and seven o'clock in the morning.

Since the confiscation of the royal family's property in 1954, some of the objects which had not been sold (sales of the family houses went on for years) can be found in an almost unknown place—namely, the third floor of the main building of the Gezira Exhibition Grounds. They include two very pleasant Delacroix flower pieces taken from Prince Youssouf's house.

Close to Prince Youssouf was Taher Pasha's house, a fine brick mansion which his cousin King Farouk bought from him and where he housed many of his collections. It is now used to receive state guests, but has retained the original owner's name and is known as the Tahra Palace.

While he was still living there, Taher Pasha had a most unhappy experience. One day, on impulse, he decided to inspect his strongroom, where he kept his gold plate: the shelves were empty. Worse still, when the culprits were eventually found, it turned out that they had melted down the objects they had stolen—a real misfortune, since the workmanship had been as valuable as the metal itself.

When the Khediva Emina asked her son Prince Muhammad Ali Tewfik to choose a place in which to establish himself, he by-passed all the palaces and houses that were at his disposal and decided on a plot of land on the island of Manial–Roda—because of a gigantic banyan tree growing there. Around that tree he designed a most beautiful garden with rare specimens that he brought back from his travels. He finally put together an important collection of palms, cacti, and tropical plants. It was a green oasis in the center of Cairo. The landscaping had been so well done that one had the impression that the place was much larger than it actually was. He himself lived in a villa built in modified Arab style beside the great banyan tree.[1] The villa holds no interest except for a room on the second floor where he placed a number of his mother's jewels and objects of gold encrusted with precious stones, as well as bedspreads and table covers also sewn with diamonds and pearls. He housed his other collections in a pleasant building constructed around an oblong whitewashed courtyard; the center of the courtyard was planted with multicolored croton shrubs, which made a fine show. This building is a little museum devoted mainly to the Middle East. Its most interesting collections are the rugs, the manuscripts, and the calligraphy. But apart from these he collected the most commonplace things that could evoke the past, ranging from old photographs to anecdotal orientalist paintings, family heirlooms, and silver or porcelain.

The Prince's library was in a solitary tower away from the turmoil of life; other pavilions were scattered throughout the garden and served various purposes. The best known is the Regency Hall, which was decorated in wild, gilded Turkish baroque. Beneath a row of windows were backless little settees, in front of each of which was placed a lovely little Turkish

---

[1] The French composer Camille Saint-Saëns was a guest of the Prince's. His Fifth Piano Concerto, 'The Egyptian,' with its pseudo-Arabic second movement, may well have been inspired by his stay.

rug. In a small room next to the Regency Hall he had placed a real museum piece, his mother's silver fourposter bed. Another room—attractive, but in my humble opinion an anachronism—had been reconstructed as an Arab drawing room.

The Regency Hall had been called by that name during King Farouk's minority because the three regents—Prince Muhammad Ali Tewfik, Aziz Izzet Pasha, and Sherif Sabri Pasha—used to meet there. Nowadays it is simply referred to as the Gilded Room. The little mosque, giving both on the garden and on the public road, is charming. The Prince used to pray there, surrounded by his household and servants, and of course anyone could step in from outside, by means of the public entrance, to join the ceremony.

The Prince bequeathed the palace, with all its contents and a grant of land to finance its upkeep, to the nation. It is now divided into two parts, of which the larger is a hotel and the smaller a government-run tourist museum and villa. The garden has been considerably mutilated by hotel accommodations—bungalows all over the place, a swimming pool, tennis courts, an open-air bar, and one of the most unnecessary and hideous fountains one could imagine. A charming pergola-walk covered with flowering creepers, one of its sides shut in by stained glass, has completely disappeared. The great banyan tree is still there, but one wonders for how much longer, given the current habit of seeing trees as wood for sale. Many of the buildings need repairing. All the same, we must be grateful to the French chain of hotels that have taken over the one half for keeping up beautifully what is left of their side of the garden—everything looks wonderfully fresh and green.

Houses changed hands with changing circumstances. Princess Chivekiar used to live close to Prince Youssouf Kemal's palace, in a spacious villa which he had lent to her. When she inherited from her brother Prince Seifeldin, she went to live in a palace opposite parliament which had been built by Ali Pasha Gelal, Aunt Iffet's husband and cousin.[1] When Princess Chivekiar died, her youngest son, Muhammad Wahideldin Selim, asked Prince Youssouf to allow him to buy the Princess's original villa, and the Prince agreed. Princess Chivekiar's son then proceeded to make

---

He was the son of Princess Zebeida, Princess Hadidja's sister, and Menelikli Pasha.

the place more palatial, installing, among other things, a splendid aubergine marble staircase. The garden was transformed, along completely formal lines, very pleasantly and successfully.

But I also noticed that among certain members of the family there was a genuine desire to reduce their life-style to a very simple one. Princess Nimet Kemaleddin (sister of Prince Muhammad Ali Tewfik), for example, moved from her palace near the Qasr al-Nil bridge, which became the Ministry of Foreign Affairs, to a villa within its grounds. At the time the building was painted a grayish-blue, which suited it; now it is a mixture of cream and beige, which somehow lacks harmony and is slightly nauseating. Another very handsome house that had also belonged to her became, in 1926, the Turkish Embassy. It was built by Princess Kiazimé, daughter of the Sultan Hussein, but at her death it was inherited by her brother Prince Kemaleddin and through him it went to his wife, Princess Nimet Kemaleddin.

Princess Hadidja Tewfik (sister of Princess Kemaleddin), on hearing that there was no hospital for tuberculosis of the bone, immediately turned over her palace at Helwan to the government for that purpose. She herself went to live in a modest house in its vicinity. Her daughter, the beautiful Princess Kérimé Abbas Halim, moved from a very normal-sized villa in Ma'adi to a tiny one, furnished with the simplest light-colored wooden furniture, everything sparkling and bright and quite spartan.

Princess Kérimé was interested in the mechanism of cars and would open up the motor of a new or unknown vehicle and peer inside it expertly. (She did this once with one of mine and I was horribly embarrassed not to be able to answer her knowledgeable questions!) She of course liked to drive her Rolls herself, her chauffeur by her side, and in private smoked cigars. She was, I thought, the best-looking person in the family, her hair turning gray very early on and her face remaining attractive, with sparkling dark eyes and a gay smile. She was married twice, the first time to Prince Osman Fuad of Turkey, and the second to Prince Youssouf Kemal, but both marriages were unsuccessful.

After living in a comfortable-sized villa in Zeitoun, Prince Ismail Daoud moved to a small, one-storied house in Matariya surrounded by a large garden of fruit trees. At the end of the garden, he stabled some horses. Opposite the house was a square lawn, with a 'Rocaille' fountain in its center. Here he entertained friends to sometimes quite large garden parties.

Muhammad Taher Pasha,[1] on leaving his palace at Zeitoun, kept a pied-à-terre in town and a house on a spur of the Pyramid plateau. The latter had a wonderful view of the Nile valley, and of the Pyramids themselves, which appeared from this vantage point like close neighbors. In summer the house enjoyed fine cool air away from the humidity of the valley. But much of his time was spent at his country house at Bordein, where he lived surrounded by his books, numerous collections of Iznik and Kutahia tiles, Chinese porcelain, and a stud of beautiful Arab horses.

The Bordein house had been built for his grandfather, the Khedive Ismail, when he once had to pass a night at Bordein on his way to Ismailia. But I think that in any case something had to be built in this region, since many members of the family who were the Khedive's descendants had lands there, including myself.

The great palaces of Qasr al-Ali, Qasr al-Dubara, Giza, and quite a few others had been demolished by about the turn of the century and their vast grounds broken up, usually for reasons of inheritance. Bits and pieces, if one looks carefully, are still to be seen, especially between Qasr al-Dubara and Munira. But soon there will remain no trace of them at all, as the façades or exterior walls are having any distinctive signs of their period carefully removed and replaced by anonymous contemporary architecture.

At Giza, in a rundown district, there is still a street called Bayn al-Sarayat—'Between the Palaces.' I was told quite lately that one of these palaces had belonged to my grandfather and the other to Prince Hussein Kamel, his brother. Prince Hussein's palace I saw when it was being used as a school; its famous gardens had already become a wasteland, with still a few trees and some indications of better days. The building was eventually pulled down and replaced by a series of disorderly sheds and houses of various sizes and colors which are today part of the arts section of Cairo University. Some years ago the handsome exterior wall of the garden underwent the usual transformation into something unattractive and inappropriate, but in its midst one of the original carriage gateways has sur-

---

[1] Son of Princess Emina, sister of Great-Aunt Nimet.

vived. Of the other palace of Bayn al-Sarayat no trace remains, and I never heard or read a description of it.

Some other palaces were abandoned for no understandable reason except, perhaps, that the district was becoming run down. Thus the Toussouns, instead of living in their very charming and spacious palace in Sharia Toussoun in Shubra, preferred to live in Aunt Behidja's (Princess Omar Toussoun) large mansion in Zamalek (Sharia Hassan Sabri Pasha), which has two other villas in its garden. The Toussoun Palace in Sharia Toussoun still exists, greatly mistreated by its present-day use as a school, but it could still be saved.

The Palace of Giza, the private home of the Khedive Ismail and the place where his son, King Fuad was born, had a completely different fate. When the buildings were demolished, the lovely gardens, still quite lovely, designed by Barillot-Deschamps, were divided in two, one becoming the Zoo and the other the Orman Garden. It was from this period, the Khedive Ismail's, that so many lovely garden and street trees were imported into the country. In the Azbakiya Garden, for example, four hundred different species were planted, of which only a few have survived.

An important social change was another reason why it was no longer necessary to have such large homes. This was the end of the institution of the harems, which had needed a vast amount of accommodation for their numerous inmates. In Egypt, harems seem to have proliferated happily in all spheres of life. The princely harems of the nineteenth century were usually enormous affairs, highly organized households, with great importance attached to precedence and rank. First came the four official wives permitted by Islam, the Four Princesses; these ladies were referred to as the First Princess, the Second Princess, and so on, as a higher form of discretion, since using their names would have been a minor intrusion into their privacy. The head of the family would maintain precedence and be treated with particular respect by everybody else, as seniority was the key word to all proceedings and ways of life of the period. An ancient grandmother completely retired from the world would have undisputed authority over any of her perhaps brilliant descendants or relatives, male or female.

After the Four Princesses came the Kadin Effendis, who enjoyed the same material privileges as the Princesses, their children inheriting and holding the same rank as those of the first four ladies. They were given their own individual households— apartments or palaces—and a personal fortune. All these ladies would be treated as respected aunts by junior members of the family who were not their descendants.

Most of these persons were of Circassian origin. Some had been brought up since childhood by members of the family with the idea of marrying them to their children later on; others were simply incorporated on account of their pleasing beauty—but not before they had been properly educated in matters of etiquette and customs. I am speaking strictly of harem habits of an Ottoman way of life in Egypt; other countries, I suppose, had or have their own proceedings. Circassians were preferred to other races not only for their physical type (which included good health, very important!), but more specifically because they were considered to have dignity, character, and natural breeding. And it is a fact that there is no record of any of these ladies having ever failed to maintain these high standards or having been disloyal to their husbands in any way.

The custom of marrying these anonymous persons was initiated by a historical incident in the fifteenth century. After the Sultan Bayazid was defeated by Tamerlane, he and his household had fallen into the hands of his foe; Bayazid was then made to attend a banquet at which his queen, a Serbian princess, was obliged to wait on the victors. To avoid any possibility that royal blood should ever again be demeaned in this manner, slaves rather than princesses were henceforth married and regarded as vessels to transmit the royal succession. Another advantage was that they had no relatives—who often might be embarrassing and ambitious! Many of these ladies were the victims of Caucasian interclan warfare; the victors pouncing upon these proud, free people—some of whom came from well-known families—and selling them off into slavery and hence into harems.

The heavy household chores in the harems, such as scrubbing floors or cleaning windows, were carried out by men or black women. (Black slaves were also prized as cooks.) Before letting the men in, all the female elements in the harems would move to another part of the house. The gentler side of things would be given over to the kalfas, who were of all ages and conditions. Each would be allotted a special task accord-

61

ing to her capacities: flower arrangements, looking after the pipes for smoking (chibouks or narghiles, the water pipes that some medical authorities now consider to be a safer way of smoking); others would be in charge of the linen room or responsible for the valuables, cash, jewelry, and plate.

Eunuchs, always black in Egypt,[1] were important factors in the harem, for they were the only link with the outside world. In Turkey, the Grand Eunuch passed directly after the Grand Vizier and held the title of Highness. In Egypt, eunuchs never attained such power and were always regarded as menials, but they were nevertheless personages to be reckoned with in the first part of the nineteenth century. Their importance, however, dwindled rapidly with the emancipation of the often high-spirited and imperious ladies of the harem until they were reduced more or less to the role of master of ceremonies, or symbolic escorts of their mistresses when leaving their homes. There is a very funny scene concerning a eunuch in A. M. Broadley's *How We Defended Arabi [Urabi] and his Friends*. I shall quote some of it, but the whole chapter entitled "Egyptian Ladies and Nationalism" is both amusing and interesting.[2] Here is the incident with the eunuch:

"Poor Princess X was sent for first [by the Khedive Tewfik] and upbraided with having written to Arabi. Her mother, however, boldly declared she had written the letter and sealed it with her daughter's seal. They were then dismissed, but the mother loudly reproached a eunuch who had accused them to the Khedive of carrying on a correspondence with Arabi, and struck him over the head with a chair, on which he ran all bleeding up the stair-case to Tewfik to make his complaint." Exit eunuch.

In some of the more important harems there could be a female orchestra belonging to the household. Hoshiar, the Khedive Ismail's mother, had

---

[1] In Turkey, there had been both black and white eunuchs. But the white ones had gradually been abandoned, since they were considered to be more corrupt than the blacks.

[2] Actually, the whole book throws an amusing light on a typical Victorian outlook on the 'natives.' The author, after extolling his client's many virtues, ends up with the words, "but he was an Egyptian and nothing more!" A.M. Broadley, How We Defended Arabi [Urabi] and his Friends: A Story of Egypt and the Egyptians. London, 1884; Cairo: Research and Pub. Arab Centre, 1980.

wo, one for European and the other for oriental music; but this of course was exceptional. She had what must have been a most charming house on he road to Helwan, which was artificially elevated so that one could see he Nile and the pyramids of Saqqara on the other shore; both orchestras would play here on summer evenings, on two terraces separated by the ength of the house.

There are some amusing descriptions in memoirs of the period of the semi-military uniforms that these lady musicians wore. Dancing girls, usually Greeks or Armenians, would come to entertain from the outside world. They would dance folk dances or create a dance on a given poetic theme. Belly-dancing was considered distasteful and unfit for private homes.

On official days the Four Princesses and the Kadin Effendis would separately receive visits from male and female members of the family. Foreign lady visitors were sometimes invited too, as is described by Miss Ellen Chennells, the governess of Zeinab, one of the Khedive Ismail's daughters:

"On the 12th of December, at sunset, the gun fired announcing the close of the long fast of Ramadan! The Princess [Zeinab, her pupil] brought me a message two or three days before, to the effect that we (Mrs. Freeland and I) were expected at the Palace of Abdeen on the first day of Bairam between ten and eleven o'clock.

"At daybreak the Khedive went to the Mosque of Muhammad Ali up by the Citadel, and a salute of twenty-three guns announced when he went in, and repeated when he came out. Then began his levée at the Citadel and after having paid their respects to him the chief dignitaries hurried off to present their salams to the Queen-Mother [Hoshiar] and the Princesses, wives of His Highness. The princes of the blood were allowed the privilege of entering the presence of these ladies; but the great dignitaries, ministers, pashas, and beys merely sent a message to each lady through the chief eunuch, asking permission to lay their heads in the dust at her feet, and receiving a gracious reply in return."

And further on Miss Chennells continues:

"The Four Wives of the Khedive were seated at a short distance from each other; they were magnificently dressed, and blazing with jewels. We were presented to each in turn, and each had something pleasant to say to us, which was duly translated by the lady who officiated as interpreter. My pupil had taught me a Turkish sentence to say to her mother, and I thought I had it by heart, but I broke down in the middle of it. The Princesses laughed and took it in very good part, so after about ten minutes' stay we rose and took our leave."[1]

The ladies of the harems would return visits to their kinswomen, and to leave their palaces they would don transparent white yashmaks, partially veiling their faces and leaving only their eyes and brows uncovered. "Most of these yashmaks were of the thinnest material, so that the face was not in the least concealed, but rather embellished. They did not hide the features so much as does the veil worn by an English lady."[2]

Adorned with jewels and surrounded by their ladies, as well as by one, two, or more eunuchs according to rank, these persons would sail forth in their smart European carriages, often driven by English coachmen and preceded by runners, who would make way for them through the unruly traffic and often narrow streets. They would be dressed in the latest European fashion, covered by light, all-enveloping coats which would be lined with fur in cold weather. On their heads they wore circular bonnets, never big but of varying heights (a matter for the wearer to decide), and these bonnets were swathed in layers of the same transparent gauze as the yashmak. The two would be pinned together low on the neck by a non precious pearl pin. On entering a house, the lady's yashmak would be removed by an attendant and, at the end of the visit, would be replaced with the help of a maid holding a richly chased, often round, silver mirror in front of the visitor, while another kalfa pinned down the veil at the back.

The yashmak survived to modern times for any official occasion when the Queen or the princesses and their ladies were appearing in public outside the Palace, except when in uniform. But it had by now become completely symbolic, as it would be draped most becomingly around the face, usually covering the tip of the chin. It was extremely flattering, like a halo around the face. For everyday use it had been completely discarded except for a very few elderly persons whom one hardly ever came across. The white yashmak, just described, is of Turkish origin and in Egypt was connected only with the palace. The traditional Egyptian veil is black and more austere.

---

[1] Ellen Chennells, Recollections of an Egyptian Princess, by Her English Governess; Being a Record of Five Years' Residence at the Court of Ismael Pasha, Khédive. Edinburgh and London: William Blackwood and Sons, 1893.

[2] Ibid.

The role of these ladies of the harems has often been underestimated. As Broadley points out, they were capable of great political influence through their husbands, princely children, or their own strong personalities. "In no part of the world do women continue to exercise so much real political power as in the East, and there is probably no oriental country in which their influence is so potent a factor in state affairs as in Egypt."[1]

Hoshiar, the Khedive Ismail's mother, was a public figure whose doings were continually reported by the press, which referred to her simply as the Queen Mother. During the Urabi revolt her patriotic feelings made her accept Urabi as the defender of the country against a British invasion. Putting aside all personal interests and the fact that he was also a menace to the dynasty, she provided him with money and horses and worked with other ladies of the family at preparing bandages and medicine for the wounded. She was a formidable person of great intelligence and character who wielded considerable influence over her son. When the Sultan Abdel Aziz of Turkey visited Egypt, he made a point of particularly honoring Hoshiar by bestowing on her the Grand Cordon of the Osmaniyeh. This beautiful and very feminine woman brought up her son with unrelenting discipline and would never allow her motherly feelings to get the better of her sense of duty, to such an extent that when the future Khedive was visiting Europe as a child, he was heard to say about the Dowager Empress of Austria, who had been particularly kind, "that no one in his own family had ever shown him as much affection." But the Khedive adored his mother and remained to the end a most devoted son.

The Queen Mother lived in her palace of Qasr al-Ali, now part of the residential district of Garden City. There she held quite incredible state, never condescending to leave her home for anyone else's, however high-ranking that person may have been. And indeed, as Ibrahim Pasha's widow and the Khedive's mother, her position was unique.

On official occasions when she was holding court, her entrance into the state rooms was a ceremony that unfailingly impressed visitors. Her maids would line the way to the throne room and, on the great crystal and bronze staircase, would be standing other kalfas—one on each step—holding lighted tapers. Her Mistress of Ceremony would appear first, richly clad,

---

How We Defended Arabi [Urabi] and his Friends.

65

holding her wand of office made of gold and studded with diamonds; then Hoshiar would arrive, always dressed in the oriental manner, and descend the staircase, some of her ladies holding her train. Followed by two young princesses, she would slowly make her way through the bowing crowds to the throne room. There she would take her place on an elevated platform while the two young princesses would sit below, one on each side of her and the ceremony would proceed, guests being led up to present their compliments and then being escorted away.

We have a short description from the English governess and her companion after they had left Abdeen and gone to call on her:

"The next thing was to drive to the residence of the Queen-Mother who lived in a palace on the banks of the Nile, which struck us as handsomer and at the same time more oriental than Abdeen. After crossing the inner courts we found ourselves in an arcade which stretched across the garden and was raised some feet above it. Two eunuchs escorted us the whole length and led us into the palace where we were received by the attendants as at Abdeen, but there was an indefinable something which looked more Eastern. The inmates were as richly dressed, but the cut of the garments was different." And a little later: "We were soon sent for into the presence of the Queen-Mother; she was not dressed in European costume, but it being a cold day, she had a beautiful Persian shawl wound round her body. She received us with a mixture of dignity and courtesy that struck us much. She looked very pleasantly at us, asked us a few questions, and then we came out again into the large saloon which we had first entered."[1]

Hoshiar was the founder of the Rifai Mosque, which is one of the main mausoleums of the royal family. The work on it continued through several reigns; its main structure was finished by 1912, but it was not completed until King Fuad's reign. Among its architects was an Austrian working for the Egyptian government, Hertz Pasha, but he simply carried out the original plans of Fahmy Pasha and was not the designer of the mosque.

I have often wondered if Hoshiar's son, the Khedive Ismail, did not inherit from her his love of splendor, for his father and grandfather were austere administrators and men of war. On the other hand, that love of splendor may simply have been in the spirit of the period (it certainly was

---

[1] Chennells, *Recollections.*

in other lands), for there are many examples of these ladies who lived in considerable state. When the mother of Abbas I, Bamba Kadin Effendi, made her entrance into Cairo in 1849, she arrived in a carriage driven by six horses, preceded by forty more carriages, each carefully shuttered, containing her ladies.

The harem was usually in a different building from the *salamlik*, or men's quarters, where the master of the house would receive visitors. The *salamlik* was a smaller and less ornate place, decently but not overluxuriously furnished in a European style. In contrast, the harems had lavished on them all the luxuries of the Orient and the western world. Nothing was too good for the inmates of this palace, the finest rugs or the latest European furniture, not always beautiful but of fine quality and now perhaps with nostalgic appeal.

On special occasions there were coffee cups of gold, embellished with enamel or precious stones—and, at the Khediva Emina's, trays completely inlaid with diamonds. Bedspreads and table covers embroidered with pearls and diamonds can still be seen at the Manial Palace Museum. In palaces other than Abdeen the chandeliers might be pastel-tinted opalines, or of white or multicolored Bohemian glass. There were rooms of carved baroque marble, and in hot weather cool water ran down the walls to form little rivulets which meandered across the floor to a central sunken fountain.[1] Baths could be of alabaster, but were more usually of white marble. In interior gardens, caged nightingales would help pass the long night away with their songs. Fourposter beds of ornate silver, with their rich, gold embroidered hangings, looked like galleons at sea. The Khediva Emina's palace at Garden City had all its fittings, even door knobs and window handles, made of silver.

In short, in the harems anything reflecting vanity, love of beauty, or splendor could be demanded by its inmates; for here amusements were a necessity and luxury an appeasement for hundreds of women who in their lifetime would know only one man and master. As Miss Chennells writes: "The Khedive [Ismail], to do him justice, was anxious to raise the position of women; he founded schools for girls, he endeavored to promote education in

---

[1] One example can be seen at the Manial Palace Museum and another, very fine, at the Military Museum at the Citadel.

his own harem, and gave much greater liberty and means, both of recreation and instruction, to its inmates than any sovereign had done before him."[1]

The more practical side of things was also not neglected. At Hoshiar's palace of Qasr al-Ali there was a permanently staffed hospital of two doctors, one surgeon, twenty male and female nurses, and a dentist to look after its over one thousand inmates. (Perhaps as a reminiscence of these customs, my father kept a resident doctor with us at Shubra, who, according to my mother, might have saved my father's life, had the foreign expert not been brought in.)

In contrast with all the above-mentioned extravaganzas, the old Zafran Palace (not to be confused with the later one) was renowned for its extreme simplicity. Built on the edge of the desert for its salubrious air, it was carpeted with multicolored reed matting and the furniture was chosen to go with the general setting.

Before leaving the subject of the harems, I would like to point out that slavery in the Near East had absolutely nothing in common with the exportation of Africans to the western hemisphere. A Frenchman travelling in Egypt in 1881 wrote: "L'esclavage est fort doux en Orient. Les mœurs qui ont quelque chose de patriarcal font de l'esclave comme un membre de la famille."[2]

And here is an impression from our much-quoted English governess upon her first stepping into a harem: "Our eyes were dazzled by what we saw. Could these gorgeously dressed ladies who came forward to meet us be slaves, of whom we had heard so much? The word SLAVE has a very different acceptation with us with what it bears in the East. There is no degradation there implied by the term. Those belonging to a great harem have generally been there since their childhood; they have no recollections of their previous life; they have grown up with the family, and identify themselves with it. They are confined, it is true, within four walls, but they are allowed a degree of liberty within those four walls, astonishing to our habits."

Islamic customs do indeed provide a number of guarantees against at least the physical abuse of slaves, including the right to ask to be sold in public to a different master if unhappy in their present house. We must

---

[1] Chennels, *Recollections.*

[2] Jean-Jacques Ampère, *Voyage en Egypte et Nubie.* Paris: Calmann-Lévy, 1881.

suppose, though, that the powerful could take advantage of their positions if inclined to do so, but never to the extent that it would reach public knowledge, since that would be an affront to respected customs that in those days nearly always originated in religion.

We have an example in one of Muhammad Ali's own daughters, the beautiful but willful Princess Nazli. Gifted with wit and intelligence she was also completely infatuated with her husband. The poor man had the misfortune one day quite innocently to admire the long golden hair of one of her maids; in a manic fit of jealousy she had the girl killed. Her husband immediately left the house never to return, and some time later she was informed that she would receive a visit from her brother Ibrahim Pasha. His mission was brief: he gave her the choice between a dagger or a cup of poison. She did not resist her fate and swallowed the poison with composure, dying in the bloom of her youth and beauty at the age of twenty-eight. A version which I heard only once, and quite recently, has it that she was imprisoned in her palace in solitary confinement, with no contact with the outside world for the rest of her life. In all fairness I have to say that the execution is the version that until now has always been considered the authentic one. For a person of her temperament, though, the prolonged suffering of years of confinement could have proved a fate worse than death. Either way the fact remains that her crime did not go unpunished.

My great-grandfather, the Khedive Ismail, was the last of Egypt's rulers to possess a harem. When he abolished slavery in his domains in 1869, it was the beginning of the end for this institution which had relied so much on women in bondage. To draw attention to the break with such an old tradition, the Khedive chose in his own inimitable way to give a spectacular example of the conduct he wished the country to follow. He married four of his children to four of their princely cousins, who were expected henceforth to live in monogamous state. They were: Tewfik, to the granddaughter of Abbas the First, the Princess Emina; Hussein, to his first cousin, Princess Ayn al-Hayat, daughter of Ahmed Pasha, the Khedive's deceased elder brother; Hassan, my grandfather, to the Princess Hadidja, daughter of the younger Muhammad Ali Pasha, and granddaughter of Muhammad Ali the Great; and, finally, Fatma, to Prince Toussoun, son of the viceroy Muhammad Said.

A week's festivities were staged for each wedding ceremony so that the whole affair lasted an entire month. The tedious, repetitive splendor of the proceedings struck the imagination of many contemporaries, who inevitably compared the happening to *The Thousand and One Nights*.

Prince Muhammad Ali Tewfik, the offspring of one of these weddings, gives an enthusiastic description of them in one of his rather quaint leaflets that he had privately printed. We are also indebted to him for some precise figures concerning the events: during four days of each of these four weeks, five hundred sheep, three hundred lambs, two hundred turkeys, eight hundred fowls, five hundred pounds of coffee, and eight hundred okes of bread were distributed daily to the poor at the Khedive's personal expense.

Apart from the ceremonies in the palaces and the public processions, the rest of the citizenry was provided with entertainment and refreshments in the city's parks. This custom of the Khedive's of including the whole of the city's population in any great festivity must have created a unique atmosphere of oneness and genuine jubilation.

The Khedive Ismail (r.1863–79) is, for some people, a controversial figure. To Lord Cromer, he was "Egypt's ruin"; to Lord Milner, he was "luxurious, voluptuous (!), ambitious, fond of display, and devoid of principles"—this of the man who was one of the richest persons in Egypt before his accession to the throne, thanks to his own intelligent enterprises, and who was twice to stay at Buckingham Palace as the guest of that paragon of virtues, Queen Victoria. Obviously the Gracious Queen must have held a different point of view from that of her cantankerous subjects. She was not the only one. To Judge Pierre Grabités, he is "Ismail the Maligned Khedive"; Edwin de Leon, the American Consul-General, writes of him: "The Khedive is an immense worker, and as it is one of the taxes on absolute power that its head must know and supervise everything, even to the minutest details, he is compelled to get up early and sit up late at the labors he loves . . . these labors and cares are beginning to tell on his health."

The British journalist McCoan writes in the same vein: "During the twelve or fourteen hours thus given to positive work for certainly more than three hundred days a year," etc., etc. And again: "He is both sovereign and minister in one—seeing everything, knowing everything, and doing everything himself." In fact the Khedive was so busy that he was reputed to have to dictate in the same room to three different secretaries simultaneously—in Arabic, Turkish, and French.

When he was prevailed upon by his family and doctors to take a holiday, he decided to sail up the Nile with only his closest family to visit the pharaonic splendors of the land. He did not get very far. At Minya he came across some sugar mills that were not functioning, and he did not move from there until they were again in working order. But by then matters of state called him back to Cairo and that was the end of his holiday. Men of repute such as Sir Samuel Baker and Gordon of Khartoum were staunch supporters of the Khedive too, and the delightful expert on Islamic Cairo, Mrs. Devonshire, calls him the Great Khedive.

This was the public image that he offered the world. In his own immediate family he was positively revered, and after his death one of his wives, Neshedil Kadin Effendi, Great-Aunt Nimet's mother, spoke of him in this manner: "Effendimiz [Effendina in Arabic, or Monseigneur] was the kindest and most considerate of men. He was far too courteous to hurt anyone's feelings and I never heard him utter an unkind word." And Great-Aunt Nimet herself to a fawning visitor: "My only pride is in being Ismail's daughter." Finally history, in judging him from a bird's-eye view, called him 'Ismail the Magnificent.'

There is little doubt that the last appellation characterizes him well; his vision of things and enterprises were always on a grand scale. Although he had received a European education, he had the oriental's love of exalting a situation to its ultimate possibilities. The Empress Eugénie wrote to her husband Napoleon III of France that her reception on arriving in Egypt for the opening of the Suez Canal was "the most beautiful thing" she had ever seen. (She herself was to make a memorable impression on a group of Egyptian court ladies who were presented to her. She was dressed all in white, with no jewels except for the famous diamond—'Le Régent'—in her hair. According to a lady whose grandmother was present at the ceremony, she was absolutely radiant.)

The Khedive's love of grandeur, apart from being a form of perfectionism, was also propaganda for Egypt, designed to put the country on the map among the modern states of the world and, from that position, to establish itself as the capital of an African empire. This goal, to a certain extent, he achieved, extending by conquest the boundaries of the Sudan to the Equatorial Lakes, converting the pagan king of Uganda to Islam (not for long), and finally abolishing the slave trade in that region in 1869. He used Sir Samuel Baker to command this expedition of Egyptian troops, who wrote to him:

"Monseigneur,

"I have the honor to inform your Highness that not withstanding the small size of the military force at my disposal, I have annexed a great part of Central Africa and the territory of Your Highness thus extends to the Equator." And further on: "Now that the slave traders are out of the country, the natives look with confidence upon the government of Your Highness."

In Europe the Khedive was beginning to be referred to as the Emperor of Africa. One cannot help but pause for a moment and wonder what Egypt would have become if the great powers of the times had thought of helping it (as they have been doing in our day), instead of seeking to profit from it. But aid to developing countries was not part of the nineteenth-century credo. Nevertheless, the progress was considerable: during the Khedive Ismail's reign arable land was increased by 50 percent—which, plus the 30 percent increase under Muhammad Ali, almost doubled its size). As to Cairo, the Khedive brought it out of the medieval city clustering around the Citadel and founded the modern town, passing through the Muski, a recent (but now decrepit) European-style section. One French tourist bitterly criticized the newly built Muhammad Ali Boulevard, likening it to "our hideous Rue de Rivoli in Paris." Innovations are rarely well received, but a more valid criticism would be that many fine old houses may have been demolished in order to build broad, straight roads, much as Baron Haussmann did in Paris at the same period.

Islamic monuments, until then sadly neglected (in fact probably the most neglected in the whole of the Islamic world), began to be restored. (On the other hand, we must not forget the destruction brought on Cairo by Bonaparte's armies, when from a spur of the Muqattam Hills, Kléber bombarded the city and specifically targeted its religious institutions.) Great credit for the restoration of mosques must be given also to the Khedive's son and grandson, the Khedives Tewfik and Abbas Hilmi II. In addition, schools, museums, and hotels (tourists complained that they were expensive) were created with an energy worthy of the Khedive's ancestor, Muhammad Ali.

At the great Paris Exhibition of 1867, the Egyptian Pavilion aroused international enthusiasm with its magnificent pharaonic treasures, which were exhibited within a reproduction of an ancient temple. The Empress Eugénie did not hesitate to ask the Khedive—on behalf of the French government—for the fabulous jewels of Queen Ahhotep, and for the rest of the antiquities displayed, including such masterpieces as the statue of the 'Sheikh al-Balad' and that of Chephren. But by then the law prohibiting the exportation of antiquities from the country had been passed, and the Khedive was able to reply quite firmly: "Madam, there is someone at Bulaq who wields greater power over these matters than myself." He was, of course, referring to Auguste Mariette Pasha, the French archaeologist who was in charge of the Antiquities Department and the Egyptian Museum, which were at the time situated in Bulaq.

Parliamentary government was introduced in Egypt in 1866 with the creation of an Assembly of Delegates. In his opening speech, the Khedive Ismail, addressing the delegates in Arabic, "referred to the great work done for Egypt by Muhammad Ali and Ibrahim, and pointed to the creation of the Assembly as a proof of his own earnest desire to continue their work. He then quoted some verses of the Quran to show that a Muslim ruler should rule by the advice of his people."[1]

In November 1881, "The Government could easily have interfered with the elections which were under the direction of its officials—the oumdas. Sherif Pasha (the Premier), however, issued a stern warning to government officials against attempting to influence the elections. *It is worth while stressing that this was the first government edict on the freedom of elections in Egypt.*" And, again, "Arabi [Urabi] and his group, though they had the power to influence the elections in their favor by force, refrained from doing so, and the people voted quite freely."[2] Professor Bernard Lewis makes the same point: "It is in Egypt that party and parliamentary government has the longest record in the Middle East."[3] The importance of these early beginnings cannot be sufficiently stressed, for I think that the technical backwardness of Egypt in comparison with western coun-

---

Landau, *Parliaments and Parties.*
Ibid. Emphasis added.
Quoted in Landau, *Parliaments and Parties.*

tries is due to its citizenry not having participated fully and in a continuous manner in its government.[1]

But the most spectacular project accomplished in the reign of the Khedive Ismail is of a different nature. The Suez Canal is so linked with his name that although the subject has been often dealt with, I feel that a word must nevertheless be said about it—which entails going back into a previous period, where it found its origins.

Muhammad Ali and Ibrahim Pasha were opposed to the project. Realizing its tremendous political and strategic importance, they feared that any move on Egypt's part would precipitate a foreign intervention that the country could not cope with. France wanted the Canal for its financial possibilities and to control the shipping route to the Far East. Britain was opposed to it for these same reasons and perhaps, too, on the principle that any enterprise favorable to Egypt's development should be nipped in the bud. In a forceful speech in parliament, Lord Palmerston announced: "It is the duty of Her Majesty's Government to fight this project." Muhammad Ali made innumerable friendly advances to England, but, much to his despair, was always rebuffed. "I know," he said, "I cannot accomplish something great without the consent of England." But the British remained adamant, as did the other great powers—all of them interested in keeping the Ottoman empire in its existing state. (This seems to have been the habitual stance of the great powers toward the Ottoman empire: witness the total agreement of Russia, Austria, and Prussia at the Münchengratz convention in 1833.) Egypt was very much on its own, with no allies, and it was this that made Muhammad Ali and Ibrahim Pasha reject the idea of the Suez Canal, a plum for any of the imperial powers. General Weygand writes: "In his wisdom Muhammad Ali refused to enter into conflict with Europe, *which traditionally has always opposed him.* His moderation, full of firmness, dignity, and grandeur, was to consolidate the basis of modern Egypt."[2]

---

[1] There is a wonderfully eloquent letter written by Prince Moustafa Fazil, the Khedive's younger brother, begging the Sultan Abdel Aziz of Turkey to give a new lease of life to the Turkish empire by introducing democracy within its frontiers. Reprinted in Cairo in 1940 by the Institut Français d'Archéologie Orientale.

[2] Général Weygand, *Histoire militaire de Mohammed Aly et de ses fils.* Paris: Impr. Nationale, 1936. Emphasis added.

But these considerations were to be swept aside by the third ruler of Egypt (if we count the simultaneous reign of Muhammad Ali and Ibrahim as one). Muhammad Said (1822–63) was Ismail's uncle and predecessor. His great friend happened to be the Vicomte Ferdinand de Lesseps, the French Consul-General. De Lesseps gained Said's friendship through one of those accidents of history which bring everything down to its lowest common denominator. As a young man Said had been overweight, and Muhammad Ali had ordered for him physical exercise and a strict diet that no one was allowed to tamper with. The only place where he could get an extra meal with impunity was at the home of de Lesseps, who plied him with his favorite food—macaroni! Thus began a great, if rather naïve, friendship. Of an openhearted and trusting nature, Said had complete faith in his friend. When he came to power, de Lesseps, who was by then in France, came back to Egypt, ostensibly to congratulate Said on his accession to the throne, but also in the hope of fulfilling his dream of obtaining the concession for the digging of the Canal. This he succeeded in doing in 1854 on a happy hunting expedition in the desert with Said, and in the bargain was given virtually carte-blanche as regards the means of carrying out the work.

Said granted such vague terms to the Suez Canal Company that—had it not been for the Khedive Ismail's subsequent efforts to modify the concession—the Company would have had almost sovereign power over the land around the Canal as well as the use of between twenty and thirty thousand pitifully underpaid fellaheen—two-and-a-half to three piasters per day for workers over twelve years old, and a piaster for those under that age. There was no proper housing or medical care; thousands died. What had been tacitly agreed upon was for a smaller labor force to be decently remunerated, the remainder of the work to be done by expensive modern machinery which the Company was supposed to provide. Swept away by de Lesseps' enthusiasm and eloquence, Said, it is said, signed the fatal document without properly reading it.

Ismail could not tolerate this quasi-colonization of Egyptian territory and abuse of his fellow countrymen. "No one is more pro-Canal than I," he said, "but I want the Canal to belong to Egypt and not Egypt to the Canal." With these words, Ismail set out to remedy his predecessor's carelessness, at great expense. He was prevailed upon to accept Napoleon III's arbitration at the Conference of Fontainebleau in 1864, when, in order to cancel the terms agreed by Said, he had to pay a preposterous indemnity.

Said was a popular ruler in his day, who was associated with the modernization of the country. To continue Muhammad Ali's policy of religious nondiscrimination, he tried—by means of an edict dated January 1856— to have the Christian population conscripted into the army along with their Muslim fellow countrymen, though this was not achieved until the reign of Ismail. I like to stress this issue because I regard these early efforts at religious liberalization of the army as perhaps one of the most important achievements of the century, without which the country would never have been able to act as a single entity (as it did so significantly in the patriotic 1920s). Ismail was fully conscious of the fact and would often refer to the religious unity of the army with pride when reviewing his troops before foreign visitors.

Said was deeply attached to his countrymen, which caused him to sponsor more officers of purely native background. The future revolutionary Ahmed Urabi was one of his young favorites, a pampered young lieutenant at seventeen, and a colonel at twenty. So one cannot help but wonder what Urabi was complaining about so much during Tewfik's reign.

Said was open-handed and generous to a fault, and his own expenses were enormous. He had huge collections of porcelain and jewelry, and at his lavish receptions even the candelabra and plate were of gold. The treasury was soon emptied, and he was obliged to borrow at a heavy rate from the Goschen Bank. To start the work on the Suez Canal he had to sell a portion of his jewelry collection, including the famous diamond 'the Pasha of Egypt,' which at one point entered a private American collection.

Like his father, Muhammad Ali, Said was a brilliant conversationalist and enormously popular with the foreign communities in Egypt, who saw in him a liberal, energetic ruler and more than a generous patron. The American Consul-General went so far as to regard him "as the finest prince in the world."[1] But I am afraid that nowadays, so far as his own countrymen are concerned, he is remembered merely as the man who allowed, to such a tragic end, the use of the corvée for the digging of the Canal. This judgment is unfair to him because as he changed from a reckless youth to a more mature man, he showed concern for the welfare of the

---

[1] Edwin de Leon, *The Khedive's Egypt, or, The Old House of Bondage under New Masters.* New York: Harper & Brothers, 1878.

peasants; he built model villages for them that he pointed out proudly (but in which the villagers stubbornly refused to live), and he passed laws in their favor in 1858 which did in fact help their lot, and for this he was gratefully known as 'the Father of the Fellaheen.'

In his last years Said was a sick and disillusioned man, racked by continuous pain. One can see in his portraits the image of someone extremely weary, but he faced death with composure and detachment, never complaining, only referring to the inevitable with a certain sardonic humor and keeping to the end his sharp wit and mind—a very different person from the impulsive young man he had been.

The Khedive Ismail, on his accession to the throne, inherited a more than doubtful situation: an empty exchequer and a national debt to a foreign bank. He was all the same to continue the work on the Suez Canal and to bring it to a historic conclusion. However, after a few years, the debts in his own reign were piling up, and in 1875 he sold his personal shares in the Canal (to Britain, the country that had been so opposed to the project!). But he was careful not to touch the 15 percent of the annual net profit of the Company that the Egyptian government was entitled to receive.

Even that small share of the profit was subsequently taken from Egypt by France and Britain, under whose joint control the country's finances were by then being administered. The 15 percent was purchased by the Crédit Foncier of France, which, in March 1880, created a subsidiary corporation called the "Société Civile pour le recouvrement des 15% des produits nets de la Compagnie du Canal Maritime de Suez attribué au gouvernement égyptien." It was after this that Lord Milner wrote, with what from this distance sounds like great satisfaction, "Egypt has no longer any share whatever in the vast profits of that undertaking."

The financial and political side of the Khedive Ismail's reign is a labyrinth quite beyond the scope of these modest family annals; but, for a general idea of the situation, we cannot do better than turn to Stanley Lane-Poole:

"Doubtless he [the Khedive] was not wholly to blame; personally he reaped small profits from his borrowings and was more robbed than robber. But while we may denounce British and French financing houses for their unblushing plunder of Egypt, we cannot forgive the ex-Khedive his share in the loans which have proved so burdensome to his country," and "Ismail's mistake lay not in the aim he set before him, but in the manner of trying to attain it. No one can doubt that he was right, as the great founder of his dynasty, Muhammad Ali, was right in striving to bring Egypt in line with European civilization . . . Ismail failed for lack of patience and judgment. He tried to rush his transformation scene. He wanted by a stroke of the pen to turn the most conservative people on earth into a living embodiment of all the virtues of a progressive and enlightened civilization."

The future Khedive had gone to Europe for ophthalmic medical care and studies in Paris, graduating from the military academy of Saint-Cyr. When visiting the different courts of Europe, he had lived in a style befitting his rank, but in Paris his student life was quite austere. Coming back to Egypt during the reign of Abbas I, he stayed away from court (one never knew on whom Abbas's wrath was to fall) and devoted his time to administering his estates, which produced the best and most sought-after crops in the land. The future Ismail the Magnificent was reputed to lead a simple, unostentatious life that impressed observers around him, and he managed his estates so well that by the time he reached the throne he had tripled his fortune. Even later, when he was accused of fantastic extravagances, his personal needs were always modest: his study in Abdeen was strictly functional, much to the surprise of visitors, just as his carriage, when he drove through town, was renowned for its elegant simplicity and his escort reduced to a strict minimum. But he himself admitted to one failing, building. He is reputed to have said: "Every man has his weakness, mine is stone."

He did away with a lot of etiquette and simplified audiences considerably. But in his family circle he was so revered that although he used to love to play and joke with his children, instinctively everyone treated him with a respect that excluded any familiarity. He was always addressed as 'Effendimiz' in Turkish, or 'Effendina' in Arabic. I always refer to him as the Khedive, although he was not to assume this appellation until sometime after his accession. His own wish had been to be called 'al-Aziz al-Masri' but this idea had to be abandoned because the Sultan in Turkey was called Abdel Aziz and took the thing amiss in a scene with his cabinet ministers.

During Said's reign Ismail was twice regent while his uncle went abroad for medical care. Foreign diplomats were quick to note his natural aptitude for government. He was a born diplomat and when he wanted to could use his celebrated charm to great effect. When, at the age of thirty-three, he went to Turkey to pay homage to the Sultan, the imperial sovereign was so completely taken with him that he decreed that henceforth he did not want ever again to have any intermediaries between himself and Ismail on any matter, either personal or relating to the state. In fact, he asked to go to Egypt to return Ismail's visit. It was the first visit of its kind since the Ottoman conquest of Egypt in 1517, but Ismail tried desperately to postpone it because the government coffers were empty and the Sultan had to be received with a magnificence in keeping with his rank. Finally, the visit took place and went off very well, the Sultan paying tribute several times to the progress the country had made under Muhammad Ali and his dynasty.

The friendliness of relations between the two rulers may have been helped by the fact that the Sultan's mother, the Validé Sultane Pertev Niyal, and Ismail's mother, Hoshiar, were sisters, thus making the Sultan and the Khedive first cousins. But blood kinship is not always conducive to friendship, especially in certain circles. Nevertheless, Ismail certainly exploited this relationship when he sent his beautiful and clever seventeen-year-old daughter, Tewhide, to Istanbul on a diplomatic mission. This she successfully accomplished, thanks to the kindness of the Validé Sultane, who treated her with great intimacy, as did all the other imperial ladies, who followed the Dowager Empress's example.

Ismail's downfall is generally explained in terms of the country's debts. This seems to me a convenient, but greatly oversimplified, explanation of a very complex situation. In this highly imperialistic period, when no bones were made about grabbing what one could (Egypt was no exception, going down to the Equatorial Lakes), Ismail was a strong personality who had to be either neutralized or eliminated; Egypt, with its Suez Canal and African empire, had become too important. The American Consul-General, Mr. E. E. Farman, wrote to his government in 1879: "It is impossible to account for the course pursued by England and France toward Egypt on purely financial grounds . . . . It would almost seem to a disinterested observer that the object was to provoke a revolt if possible, to have an excuse to take possession of the country."

To overcome the country's financial crisis (a ridiculously small sum by today's standards), the Khedive offered all his personal fortune and the most liberal parliamentary constitution, whereby he would become a purely constitutional monarch. This was not at all what the foreign powers had in mind: they sent him their favorite Egyptian statesman, Nubar Pasha, with a proposal that he keep his enormous personal fortune but relinquish the reins of government to a Franco-British rule with no Egyptian participation. Of course the Khedive refused this cold-blooded proposition, and it was then that the axe fell. Pressure was brought on the Sublime Porte, well orchestrated by the Khedive's own enemies at Istanbul; thus he received the famous or infamous telegram from the Sultan, who was still the nominal suzerain of the Near East, depriving him of his functions. With the main international military powers armed against him, and the Egyptian army forcefully reduced by the same powers after Egypt's victory at Nézib, no resistance was possible, and Ismail handed over the reins of government to his eldest son Tewfik. Two years later Egypt was a British colony. It was a brilliant international triumph, but a disastrous setback in the country's historical evolution.

One of the minor effects of this change of power was the extraordinary increase of civil servants in the government. Between 1882 and 1907 the number increased by 85 percent. This growth in the civil service has been laid at the door of the British, who liked to have everything signed and countersigned at different levels.

For the family, the takeover by the British was to be a most critical moment, a turning point. Princes, no longer allowed to participate in government, were reduced to honorific positions, with only a few philanthropic activities open to them. In their place, a new, more pliable class was to emerge. The heads of state themselves were to endure continuous minor or public humiliations to remind them of their changed circumstances.

Tewfik found himself virtually reduced to a puppet and lost some of his popularity. But this I find very harsh, since I do not see what a man in his position could have done. He was always dignified and presented to the public the image of a respectable family man.

His son, Abbas Hilmi II, was to show a more independent spirit. His patriotic aspirations were to result in the British deposing him in 1914. The throne was then offered to his uncle, the Prince Hussein Kamel, who refused it twice, stating that the rightful sovereign was his nephew, Abbas Hilmi. He was offered it a third time and was informed on this occasion that, if he did not accept, there would be a change of dynasty, and that the British candidate was waiting at Shepheard's Hotel! He then agreed to become the Sultan Hussein—enormously popular and a brilliant speaker with a gift for extemporizing speeches in Arabic. His early death was to avert the possibility of another crisis of the Abbas Hilmi kind. I had always thought that he came to a natural end, but according to a source so close to the Sultan that I cannot ignore it, he was given an injection of tubercular microbes that curtailed his life.

It was only Fuad who was able to start pulling the country out of the abyss into which it had fallen.

There are few lonelier situations than a man's fall from power. Yet when the Khedive Ismail was deprived of his throne, the Palace of Abdeen was not deserted, but was instead filled with people who had come to express their loyalty and sympathy for him.

By 1879 Ismail had bequeathed to the country his private fortune of 430,000 feddans, and the princesses, his wives, quite independently insisted on donating all their jewels, so that not the slightest blemish could fall upon his name. His children, too, handed over part of their estates for a stipulated amount of time, ten years I believe, so that their revenues would help finance the government; but these lands were never returned to them, and it was always considered that Great-Aunt Nimet lived in relatively straitened circumstances in comparison with what her original fortune had been.

We, too, were to be deprived of the palace of Gezira, where my grandparents had been living. The palace was to pass through many phases: the grounds were broken up, the main building was reduced, one important pavilion, the *salamlik*, was burned to the ground through negligence. The palace then became a hotel, and finally ended up in the possession of a well-known Levantine family with whose name it is often associated. One of the owners very kindly allowed me to visit it. I found it had no appeal for me, although I was sometimes taken aback when confronted with family portraits staring down at me. For Aunt Aziza it was a painful subject, as she had been born there, and she had her chauffeurs instructed never to pass by it if it could be avoided.

Miss Chennells, our English governess, called this palace—with poetic license— the Versailles of Egypt. Its grounds extended to where the Cairo Tower now stands, and when Princess Faiza, King Farouk's sister, went to live in a house close by, an old apricot tree, which had survived inactive from Ismail's days, suddenly burst into bloom.

The Fish Grotto in Zamalek had also been part of the palace. Its very obviously artificial hill had been built when one of the ladies of Ismail's family had complained of the flatness of the land. Today the palace, completely transformed, has been incorporated into a hotel building.

On seeing the reduced financial situation of his family, the Khedive besought the government, before he stepped down, to provide them with enough to live on decently; but it goes without saying that this plea was never given consideration.

The Khedive had wanted to settle down on his estates in Turkey, but the Sultan refused him entrance to his lands. In the last years of his reign, the Khedive could not afford to go to Istanbul because of the costliness of the presents expected there. On his last departure from Turkey, at a loss for a parting gift for the Sultan, Ismail left him—among many other things—one of the three yachts he had come with. The lack of funds to slake the thirst of the imperial sovereign and his court may have well contributed to the Khedive's downfall.

King Umberto of Italy now steps in, a most redeeming figure; he very chivalrously offered the deposed Khedive asylum in his own land, putting at his disposal the palace of 'La Favorita' at Naples, which was gratefully accepted. The Khedive asked to depart from Egypt as an ordinary citizen with no ceremony, yet the sorrowing crowds that followed him to Cairo station were an eloquent tribute to him. From there he went on to Alexandria to board the state yacht, the *Mahroussa*, for exile. Here again the crowd of dignitaries who had come to escort him aboard expressed their grief, many of them quite openly in tears. Although visibly moved, the Khedive remained sufficiently his usual considerate self to have a kind word for everyone present.

He died in 1895 after a long and painful illness which left him completely wasted. A few months before his death he sent a pathetic photograph of himself to Egypt, asking to be allowed to die in his beloved land. Yet his prestige was still such that the anxious and perhaps also callous authorities (the Prime Minister was Nubar, his avowed enemy), fearing a last-minute popular uprising, refused the dying man's wish. Death finally came to him in his beautiful palace on the Bosphorous at Emirgan, surrounded by his devoted family, for whom his person was sacred.

His body rests at the mosque of Rifai next to his mother Hoshiar. Two of the princesses, his wives, survived him and were allowed to return to Egypt, where they built the second Zafran Palace. They lived there together, by their own wish, thus keeping going to the last the remains of Ismail's household. Princess Ayn al-Hayat Ibrahim, who stayed at Zafran as a ward of the last remaining princess, Djananiar, described life there as traditional, with a lot of kalfas and eunuchs, and education formal and strict. The palace itself was handsomely appointed in a completely European style, with many portraits of foreign crowned heads hanging in the main hall. A staircase led from there to the first floor, where there was a large and beautifully kept conservatory filled with exotic plants and flowers. But this first floor could also be reached by a lift.

Life at Marg with Great-Aunt Nimet, the last surviving daughter of Ismail, preserved, as one may well expect, many of the customs of the Khedive's times, though simplified. But to us children, used as we were to family life at Shubra and San Remo, these customs seemed a little far-fetched and formal. For instance, to greet our great-aunt in the morning, every step was calculated like a choreographic scenario. Accompanied by Miss Machray, we would leave Uncle Ala'adin's house, cross the grounds to the rose garden, where a gardener would be waiting for us to choose one flower each, which he would cut for us. We would then proceed to the main house, up the steps into the hall, to be saluted by bowing kalfas, turn to the right into a small drawing room or ante-chamber, and then into our great-aunt's boudoir, with her bedroom in the background.

We would find Great-Aunt Nimet seated in an armchair facing the door, on each side of her small tables, covered with books, writing pads, and pens and pencils. She would be perfectly groomed (I never saw her otherwise), in a floor-length dressing gown, with perhaps a kalfa on a footstool at her feet, massaging a stockinged foot, or another of her women kneading the back of her neck. We would advance according to age, eldest first, kiss her hand and raise it to our brow while simultaneously she would be kissing us on both cheeks and we would finish with a *téménah*. Taking our flowers, she would hand them over to a waiting kalfa, who would put them in water and place them on a table. We would sit in armchairs opposite hers, not leaning back too far, hands folded in our laps, and ankles crossed.

There were of course variations on this theme: if one had done something to displease, there would be only one kiss on one cheek; something worse, no kiss at all, just the hand; something bad, not even the hand, just a severe look of recognition; and, even worse than this, a glance while proceeding with whatever she was doing. But in normal circumstances she would talk to us very pleasantly, and we would answer but not initiate a conversation. If there was something we wanted to ask, we would consult Miss Machray beforehand, who would on her own authority give us permission to do so, or she would inquire first of Great-Aunt Nimet if what we wanted to say was suitable and then tell us to go ahead.

After about a quarter of an hour, Great-Aunt Nimet would let us leave. To begin with it all seemed very formal, but soon it became the natural thing to do, especially since such observances were more or less the normal procedure in most branches of the family between the younger and the older generations of both sexes. When I was introduced to my little cousin Faizy, who was four years younger than myself, he kissed my hand, and I, not knowing better and not to be outdone in politeness, kissed his—to the general amusement of everyone present.

My brother Ismail was the only one who, when in trouble, could get around Great-Aunt Nimet's forbidding manner. He could be extremely funny, and it was difficult to resist his antics. One day after luncheon we were all sitting together in the small drawing room next to the dining room. There were always a few minutes of silence while Great-Aunt Nimet made a murmured prayer of thanks for the food received that day, after which the conversation would become general—except, on this occasion, for Ismail, who for some reason or other was in disgrace and was supposedly being ignored by our great-aunt. But she could not resist glancing in his direction from time to time, where he sat with such a droll air of mock penance that finally she began to laugh and all was forgiven if not forgotten.

Chapter Five

Turkey and England

The ship glided silently into the bay of Izmir. The sky was overcast, and the water dark gray with patches of deep green. Hills enfolded in an irregular movement the city of Izmir, or Smyrna, and its spacious bay. On the waterfront, as one approached land, one could see grim warehouses and modern buildings painted a bluish gray; but beyond the conventional modern city, little cobbled streets wound their way upward between picturesque wooden houses until they reached the crest of the hill, surmounted by its imposing castle.

On the other side of the hill I was to find some of the happiest days I was to know. Accompanied by Miss Machray, I was journeying toward International College at the little village of Kizil Çulu, half an hour inland by train from Izmir. There I was going to stay with the Reeds, an American family I was going to adopt as my own. I will not embarrass them with personal descriptions, except for Mrs. Reed, whom one cannot pass over in silence, as will attest all who have known her.

Born Rosalind MacLaughlan, she was the daughter of the Rector of International College, who was a friend of my uncle, Mahmud Mouhtar Pasha. Mouhtar Pasha would often come to International College, and as a young girl Rosalind would play for him on the college organ. She married Dr. Cass Arthur Reed, a professor at the college, and they had three children: Lauchlan, then studying in America; and Howard and Joan, who were at Kizil Çulu. All three were older than I, Joan, the youngest, being just one year older.

For me, Rosalind Reed was the soul of the family. Although never domineering, her presence could be felt all around one. Her sense of duty was completely inherent in her and her happy disposition—full of fun and cheerfulness—in no way impaired a dignity which was always as much present as her other qualities. Ready to help any cause or person in need, of all creeds and nationalities, she was also a most gifted person. Her greatest accomplishment was her piano playing, which was of a completely professional standard, with a fine, rich tone to it, never hesitant or lacking in depth. Apart from this, she had all the interests that a highly cultured and at the same time energetic person can have. To her and Asia Minor, with its fabulous historical past and extraordinary natural beauties, I am very much indebted, and I was quick to sense what an exceptionally lucky person I was to find myself in the midst of such circumstances and people.

We lived in a house on the campus which had some fine old family pieces of furniture, two beautiful three-quarter grand Blüthner pianos, and lovely Turkish rugs. There was also a square table covered by a gray quilt reaching to the ground. Underneath it was a brazier, which contained burning charcoal of a special nonsmoking variety. In cold weather one could draw up a chair and sit, Turkish peasant fashion, the quilt tucked over one's knees. (This custom also seems to occur in other countries, in Japan for instance, but there people sit closer to the ground.) At a little distance from the campus was the farm, where on hot days we would swim in the waters of a stone cistern. Nearby we used to run across a fine Roman aqueduct that spanned a steep little valley, its almost dry riverbed dotted with shallow pools of green water.

In an enclosed field browsed Mahpoop, a handsome, white Anglo-Arab horse that I learned to ride. He was very sensitive and would be quite gentle with children, yet frisky and full of fun with grown-ups. When I would go up to the enclosure, I would call him and he would trot over, neighing gently, and nuzzle me with his silky gray nose. He remains one of my favorite encounters in life, and his presence is as real as that of any good friend whose memory I cherish. Our favorite ride was to a hill outside Kizil Çulu covered with olive trees with, at the summit, one solitary cypress. We would tell Mahpoop, "Go to the old cypress tree"—and off he would go, cross the village, take the little path up the hill through the olive groves and stop at the old cypress tree. There one evening after sunset, in the graying light, I saw a blue bird the size of a crow, a bird I have never seen again.

In spring the hills would bloom into a carpet of anemones and cyclamen, the biggest and most beautiful I have ever seen. Flowers were abundant in that part of the world (the tulip and carnation have become an emblem of

Turkish art), and one of our excursions was to admire a field of peonies close to the little village of Kemal Pasha further inland, which we reached by train. The wooden houses of the village elbowed each other around a cobbled square, shaded by old plane and chestnut trees. In the center of the square was a stone fountain fed by sparkling water that came tumbling down in a cascade from higher ground. Crossing the little square, we were to start up the mountainside, with beside us cherry trees laden with fruit, to which the dour but hospitable local peasants invited us to help ourselves.

A gentle drizzle had started to fall, and there was some talk of leaving us children in an open wooden shelter encountered on the way, but we all protested and carried on well up into where the woods started. There, like some mythological surprise, we came upon a clearing covered with large red peonies with golden hearts, as in a Chinese painting. Yet there was also something sad and bedraggled about the scene, as if these peonies were the last of a species forgotten by time. The drizzle had stopped, but the woods were rich with moisture and the light remained hazy around us. The only sound came from the cracking of twigs among the trees and our voices sounded loud and foreign to the place. An uncomfortable feeling crept over me as if we were intruding on something private or very ancient, and only left me when we reached the homely village below, with its old gentlemen sitting in their modest café, blue smoke emerging from hidden chimneys, and the rustic smell of burning wood to greet us.

At Christmas time we drove quite far into the countryside in search of mistletoe with which to decorate the house. We found it growing as a parasite on barren trees, the white luminous berries gleaming in the reflected light of the snow. On the way back, when it was already dark, it was bitterly cold and snowing hard, and as we passed through a village we caught a fleeting glimpse of people watching two camels fighting in a field by torchlight.

The ruins of Ephesus, with their masses of marble and stone set in the incandescent summer countryside, made another memorable day. During the drive back on white, dusty roads, we stopped to bathe in the sea by an olive grove strewn with pieces of antique marble. In an adjoining field wild wheat, dotted with red poppies, unfurled itself beneath billowing clouds and a gentian blue sky.

But it was not all excursions and play. There were lessons too. English and Turkish and the usual things a child has to endure. All was torture, since I hated the discipline of laboring through subjects I had no affinity with. Compensation was listening to Rosalind Reed and Cecil La Fontaine playing on the two pianos—glorious music that I was being initiated in. It seems strange looking back, but I remember quite distinctly not understanding anything of Rachmaninoff's Second Concerto, which sounded like a turbulent confusion of notes, while Haydn, Bach, and Schubert were quite clear and crystalline to me.

Another novelty, of a very different nature, was being introduced to some very delicious American cooking!—the best ice cream I have ever had, lemon pie, strawberry shortcake, fudge, and cookies, which have all remained my favorite desserts till now.

The Reeds were forced to make a painful decision, to leave their well-loved Turkey and move to Beirut. Among other sentimental problems was having to dispose of Mahpoop; he was finally given to the mounted police of Izmir.

On the way to Lebanon we spent the summer in Greece, again an unforgettable experience, camping by the sea at Vugliarmeni, visiting the Peloponnesus, Mycenae, Corinth, lovely Aegina, and Sunium. There, among its colonnades of marble, we witnessed the majestic rising of the moon out of the sea. Twelve years later, visiting the Reeds in Athens, we were all privileged to enjoy a complete repetition of the scene: again, as if by magic, the heavy yellow moon rose among the white columns of the temple while everything else receded into the background.

Beirut had certain things in common with Turkey: the cyclamen, the anemones, primroses too, but not so numerous, not so beautiful; a lovely countryside but looking cramped between mountain and sea in comparison with the beginning of the steppes of Asia which we had just left. All the same, the drive up to the Cedars was spectacular, and so was Baalbek in the spring—the splendid, ornate temple architecture set against distant snow-capped mountains, while young fruit trees in bloom were like an annual offering to the altar of Jupiter. A quick journey to Jerusalem under snow at Christmas was moving, as was the gentle rolling countryside going to Bethlehem.

One afternoon in Beirut, Mrs. Reed called me aside and said she had something important to talk to me about. I could see she was really upset and she immediately came to the point. She had just received instructions from Cairo that she could not comply with and she thought it might mean my having to leave them. She was quite right: the matter was not taken up again, but some time later it was quietly decided that I should leave for school in England.

The whole thing had been too good to last much longer, and thus ended those very happy days, for which I must always be grateful. Just lately, as I was sorting out some papers, I came across a very solemn farewell letter from Howard Reed, telling me that my stay with them had been a very useful thing, as it had taught them to be kind to others. For me this encounter outside my own family was to leave me with the illusion that everyone in the world was kind and beautiful. I was to go on through the years carrying this time bomb with me, only to have it triggered off quite recently by people who of course I had every natural reason to trust. What a surprise it was! But I cannot complain of my naïveté or plain mental obtuseness, for while the illusion lasted, it was to take away the sting of many minor calamities and shield me from much unpleasantness.

Arriving in England was a strange experience. I had the feeling of already having lived there before and everything seemed terribly familiar: the streets, the people, what was coming around the corner, the smells of the city in particular, the air—nothing was new. Whereas I had loved Turkey and Greece, this was simply coming home.

I was met there by Miss Machray's charming and attractive niece Edna, who accompanied me to Eton. We visited the school on a somber day with forbidding clouds heavy with rain. The buildings were empty, since it was out of term, and I remember just one high, dark hall which was particularly gloomy and also a very wet, gray courtyard.

But next day I was whisked off to Leighton Park, a school near Reading. No explanation was forthcoming, and it remained one of the many minor—and, if I may say so, irritating—mysteries which cropped up for me in those days. In the long run, it was really terribly unsettling to be never even superficially consulted or told what was happening to one. (In this case I was finally to learn the reason why many years later, and the explanation was so ludicrous that I will not put it down here.)

My home at Reading was to be with one of the professors of the school and his family. Again I was particularly fortunate to be accepted by such kind, nice people as Dr. Reginald Robson, his wife Mary and their four sons Herbert, John, Peter, and Pat. They were Quakers, or Friends, a united musical family who differed from others in the neighborhood by going to Meeting instead of Church on Sundays. They lived in a house of red brick with a gravel courtyard in front, dominated by a dark monkey tree. On the right-hand side was a wooden trellis with climbing white roses and a bed of red and yellow tulips which separated the courtyard from a little formal garden with paths winding among flower beds and shrubs—a rather sad little place. The back of the house gave on a square lawn with a few apple trees, a greenhouse, and a shed where we kept our bicycles. From my spacious front bedroom I could look across the geometrical movement of the monkey tree's branches to the tall pointed spire of Christ Church, just across the street, a remarkably silent house of worship, from which only on Sundays could voices be heard in hymn singing.

For a couple of years I was a day-boy at Leighton Park, cycling there or taking a red bus which stopped in front of the school, a lovely place, its grounds roughly shaped in the form of a triangle. Its pupils came from a variety of backgrounds: there were some prominent names, among them Cadburys and Rowntrees, and two or three foreigners present, but it was not 'Establishment,' as was Eton. There was no fagging, no corporal punishment, and the presence of one or two boys from the less well-off families of the town helped ensure contact on all social levels. From my experience there, I was to retain a sincere admiration for the Quakers of England, with their sensible, dignified, and broad-minded ways.

The school consisted of one modern building and three houses for boarders: Groves, School House, and finally my own house, Reckitt. To reach it, I would cycle through a lane of elm trees, and pass the pond, which was covered with reddish acquatic weeds, where we would search for newts and other horrors. I would then pass an old abandoned farmhouse on my left and finally come to the green playing fields that stretched in front of Reckitt. On each side of the house were rhododendron bushes, and to its right a handsome cedar tree stood at the edge of the surrounding woods.

As usual the discipline of school hours, of mathematics and science, were hard on me. I caused a minor scandal during a chemistry class when the exasperated teacher, in an effort to make me understand what must have been a fairly simple experiment, asked me, "How do you make a cup of tea?" When I had to admit that I did not know, a horrified murmur of disapproval rose from the class. I must have been a problem to my teachers, for some favorable reflexes to subjects I liked, plus the advantages of a little traveling, would buoy up their hopes—only to have them dashed to the ground in subjects where these were of no help. On the other hand, hobbies were encouraged, and at least two were compulsory. I rushed headlong into them, piano, painting, pottery, carpentry, and book-binding, the first two being my real interests.

In sports I loved rugger (wing three-quarter), but running the 'Triangle' (the school boundaries), which was also quite rightly inflicted as a punishment, was a real ordeal. Cricket, too, I was not very keen on, although there the lounging about in agreeable surroundings and summer weather gave a pleasant side to it. My great treat came once a week when I was allowed to go riding. I loved horses, but was also very nervous with them. What was strange is that in these circumstances I insisted on going on with it. At Kizil Çulu, dear old Mahpoop had been a friend on whom I would dash about without the slightest apprehension; now, except on the most well-mannered ponies, I was quite nervous. Then one summer I went to Bavaria for the holidays, and as usual demanded to go riding. What happened I cannot explain, but I came back completely changed. My riding teacher, a charming woman, could hardly believe her eyes; she started to give me more exciting mounts, got me going on jumping, and everything from then on was quite different and for the better. I suppose it must have been one of those metabolic changes which are the mysteries of childhood.

The weather, which was an everyday topic, did not bother me, although I remember counting forty days and nights of either rain or drizzle. In my bedroom there was only a little heating in the morning, and a window always partially open at night. When I became a boarder at school, regulations prescribed cold baths every morning, and that one present oneself wet and naked to a prefect for inspection at the other end of the house. When the weather was really cold, the water would freeze in the pipes and, to avoid this, lighted candles would be placed next to them at night.

During the summer holidays I would join my great-aunt, Ismail, and my sisters in Europe, usually Munich, Garmisch-Partenkirchen, Eibsee, Vienna, Kitzbühl, or watering places like Bad Kissigen. But the summer of 1939 was considered unsafe and I spent the holidays with the Robsons at a little Cornish village by the sea. There, at the end of a beautiful day with everyone listening anxiously to the radio, we heard the declaration of war. For me, born in 1924, the word was unreal, something that happened to others, in history, not to human beings of our generation. I simply could not imagine people starting to kill each other on government orders. But from the expression on the older persons' faces I understood that something terrible was afoot that no one could avoid. And indeed the Robsons, like many other families, were not to be spared great suffering. Peter and John were to be the victims.

Henceforth there was to be an irrevocable change: Asia Minor would never be as lovely again, Epidaurus as magical, or buttercups in a field or bluebells in a wood as innocent. Pollution, moral or real, had set in.

The end of the holidays came—back to school, to the blackout, air-raid warnings, rationing, fewer sweets at the tuck shop—and an end to my newly inaugurated and short-lived smoking parties for two or three special friends, when we puffed at Russian Sobrani cigarettes behind the hedge of the 'Colonel's' garden. After these amenities were no longer to be had, we were too grand to go for anything that we considered inferior!

School Certificate lay ahead, which meant less riding and less music. Winning a piano competition with encouraging comments was passed over in silence in Cairo; extra math lessons were ordered, together with Arabic and Turkish, to be given, as usual, by outside professors. A complete waste of time, since by now I was forgetting everything except English.

Everyone was knitting for the armed forces, so I had a try, most unsuccessfully, at making a scarf for the R.A.F. The width seemed to augment and diminish uncontrollably, finally producing an elongated piece of wool, which at best could have been used for polishing doorknobs!

Reading turned out to be quite a safe place while I was there. Although we had a few air-raid warnings, I cannot remember any bombing. I was just as happy during as before the war, for by now I had grown deeply attached both to Leighton Park and to the Thames valley area, with all its delights for a growing schoolboy: rowing and swimming, long walks on the downs, bicycling and riding through the unspectacular, but lovely, countryside. So when I was summoned by my housemaster, Mr. Nicholson, in the middle of my examinations and told I was leaving for Egypt in three days' time, it was a thunderbolt out of the blue. I begged to be allowed to stay on at least long enough to finish my exams, but to no avail. Orders from Egypt were formal: I was to leave on the SS. *Madura* from London in three days' time, and neither my housemaster nor the headmaster, Mr. E.B. Castle, could help me out.

I was desperate; and later on, to my sorrow, I was to learn that the Reeds had offered to have me come to California and finish my studies there. How different everything would have been! But fortunately at the time I knew nothing of this; otherwise my feelings of frustration would have been complete. So I gave away my few personal possessions to my friends—my bicycle, gramophone, classical records, books—and to the charwoman who used to do my room at the Robsons I gave my most treasured possession, a small, red Bohemian glass vase with gold encrustations depicting elephants and palm trees, a present from Aunt Emina. I thought it might come in handy if ever the lady were in need of money—I had none myself, my pocket-money being set by Cairo to accord with the average allowance of the other boys at school, which was something quite small.

The SS. *Madura* sailed out of the Thames estuary with a convoy to the North Sea (the Channel was too dangerous to negotiate at the time). There we immediately got a taste of warfare when a submarine alert was sounded. All we were ever to know of it was the sound of depth charges going off at quite a distance from us; but a hit must have been made, as oily patches were reported on the sea's surface. We continued up to Scotland, parting there with the convoy, which was moving east, we supposed to Russia. Rounding the coast of Scotland, I was struck by the extraordinary purity of the evening colors—reds, greens, blues—each one distinct and not merging into the others.

We zigzagged south across the Atlantic; at one time we were so close to America that we thought we might go through the Panama Canal into the Pacific, but our first port of call was Freetown, where, in its bay, we had an extraordinarily exotic golden sunset over muddy waters.

From Freetown we went on to the Cape, running so short of water on the way that it had to be kept for drinking use only. There was little to do aboard except to swim in a small canvas pool; admire the long Atlantic swell, where, in the depth of its trough, the old ship would creek and shudder as if incapable of climbing out of it again; and, luckily for me, there was a piano on which I could practise. We had several German submarine alerts, but they spared us—preferring, I was told later, to sink the poor *Madura*, with its nice Far Eastern crew, on its way back to England laden with more precious and vital cargo than ourselves.

From Cape Town to lovely Durban was but a short journey. There we were most hospitably entertained. On board ship we had been quite a numerous group of Egyptians, as some had been at Oxford or Cambridge. Among them was Mounir Sabri, son of the then acting Prime Minister, Hassan Sabri Pasha, who was to die so dramatically while addressing parliament.

I was very kindly received in Durban by Colonel Campbell and one of his beautiful daughters, who was married to a British naval officer. The Indian community, too, was most gracious, giving us a splendid lunch at their lovely country club. This was followed by a meeting in a hall in town. We were seated garlanded with flowers on the platform, and the chairman made a welcoming speech which gradually turned to politics. Mounir Sabri answered with his usual panache, starting with normal formalities, sympathizing with their problems (apartheid), and then in a sudden change of mood berating them violently for not reacting more energetically. The audience began to get restless, some not appreciating the criticism and others, on the contrary, getting all worked up and enthusiastic about it. But the stalwart, blond Military Police at the back of the hall, certainly the best-looking people I have ever seen, remained calm and impassive.

Then to my horror I heard voices from the crowd calling my name. I am afraid I was a complete wet blanket and disappointment to most. I got up, and somehow, to my surprise, words came to me quite naturally; having thanked the people in the audience for their welcome, I suggested that enough had been said about politics, and thus I broke up the meeting. Not all were hotheads, and some congratulated me for stopping what might have become trouble. On my arrival in Cairo, I received a letter from the Indian community asking me to send them an Egyptian flag; this I was unable to do, since my elders (to whom I handed over the request) did not find it opportune.

After the meeting we gave a cocktail party to thank everyone for their hospitality. It was also to be the parting of ways from my fellow travelers, with whom I had voyaged for forty-four days from England. I now proceeded on my own by imperial flying boat to Mombasa, the Equatorial Lakes, Khartoum, where I spent the most incredible of hot nights, and finally Cairo. I could not believe that I was finally coming home. I had left Egypt as a child and now here I was, over sixteen years old. I was coming back excited and full of interest, but I have to admit with some misgivings.

Chapter Six

Cairo

The flying boat splashed down on the Nile at Rod al-Farag gurgling and spluttering on the brown waters; it finally calmed itself to a grudging silence and we were allowed to land.

A little group of persons was waiting for me, among them—standing half a pace back from the others—my mother, looking at me with anxious eyes. I did not notice anyone else, but went straight to her. After I had embraced her, she kept on scrutinizing my face and then my left hand, where I had had a scar since childhood. Later on she told me she had not been sure it was me who had come off the flying boat, as I had changed so much. I had forgotten my Italian, a childhood language, most of my French and Arabic, and only my English was fluent, which we never used among ourselves. And, physically, instead of a straight nose I had by now developed a strong aquiline one! For me she was the same being I had missed so much for so long: the warm, expressive eyes, the plump, well-shaped hand with the big, flat round emerald which so often went with it; even her style in clothes had remained reassuringly her own.

Hadidja, Aicha, and Miss Machray formed the rest of the group. Hadidja had changed a lot. Married and divorced, she was now independent, with a home of her own, and her sophisticated elegance was a far cry from the no-nonsense dresses of her childhood. Aicha was more mature, but still her own composed self, with her pink-and-cream complexion, blue eyes (like our paternal grandfather), and fair hair. Tall, straight, and smiling, Miss Machray was the same as ever, emitting a feeling of strength and security that was lacking in all of us dispersed persons.

It was strange meeting each other in this unfamiliar part of the city, surrounded by a suburb of minor factories and slums; only the Nile was its usual majestic self, rolling on, ignoring both mortals and the land it had created. After a while we took leave of our mother and helped her to her car. Aicha and I then got into the front seat of Hadidja's red Dodge, which she was driving herself, and Miss Machray followed tactfully alone in Aicha's chauffeur-driven dark-blue Buick.

Once out of Rod al-Farag, the familiar streets came back to me much as I had remembered them, friendly, casual, sun-bleached, with ornate art-nouveau or turn-of-the-century villas in usually untidy gardens. At Zeitoun we passed by Taher Pasha's house, immaculate in the rundown district, but with other very handsome houses close by, a few actually built on sandy soil with scattered palm trees for a garden. Next to these, on the desert itself, a horse market was in progress on each side of the road, the animals loitering or rolling in the sand, others being led out of white-washed or pink stables with violet bougainvillea spilling over the court-yard walls.

Rubbing shoulders with the horse market stood the stately beige pile of Prince Youssouf Kamal's Palace at Matariya. Close to it, an elongated gar-den of fruit trees, following the line of the road, marked one of my father's bachelor residences, where he had lived in a small house to be close to rel-atives he was fond of, and also to be near the desert for riding. After cross-ing a railway line, the countryside proper started with, on the right, Sir Wilfred Blunt's domain, a big garden of mango trees surrounded by a thick mud wall; on the left, a house set among orange and lemon groves was where the author of *Via Mala* lived with his two daughters, who used to come to visit my sisters at nearby Marg.

Marg, we were almost there, a bridge spanning a canal and again a rail-way crossing, and we were finally in the great palm forest, with the black, shrouded women at their place by the village pump. Driving dangerously fast, we flashed through the village, leaving behind us fluttering poultry in a turmoil of dust, leisurely peasants at their cafés, and a sheikh jogging along contentedly on his donkey, holding over his head a white umbrella lined in green. Again into the green and yellow fields, with an abandoned water-wheel next to a clump of trees on our left and, on the other side of the road, irrigation ditches lined with poplar trees planted by Uncle Ala'adin. Beyond the fields one could see the golden sand dunes of the desert. The poverty-stricken, gray *izba* of Marg rushed toward us and suddenly we were there, at the garden entrance, with the two porters in dark blue robes bowing us into the hedgebound avenue leading to the main house.

Marg, back to Marg. Nothing had changed, the gardens were lovelier than ever, the sky serene. There was Béchira running toward us in his black frock-coat to open the car's doors, kissing my hand and uttering many *ma sha' Allah*s ('The Lord be praised') in his high-pitched voice, welcoming me back in flowery Turkish. In the house were Konja, an enormous black woman with huge buttocks, a woman of authority; Pervin, Turkish, small, and thin; and the 'Poetess', a slender, genteel lady who moved with the ethereal grace of a column of smoke and earned her keep by predicting pleasant fortunes in the dregs of coffee cups and making old-fashioned Turkish poems. And all the other kalfas and men servants.

Aunt Nimet appeared to have aged a little. She walked with less energy, but her personality seemed to have remained unchanged—smiling, gracious, magnetic, but, as always, with something a little distant.

When night came, I listened to the silence of the place, the perfume of the surrounding fruit groves in bloom rising into the house, into my room. All was breathlessly quiet, except for the night watchmen, who, dispersed at intervals in a circle on the edge of the garden, would every hour signal to each other by coughing quite loudly and yet somehow discreetly, "Ahem, Hem . . . mm." From Uncle Ala'adin's house one of these signals was quite audible, since it was close to one of the garden boundaries, but the second would be much farther along, the next more distant still, until at some point the sound got completely lost. Then it would come back by stages to its point of departure, and again all would be silent for an hour in the big garden.

My studies were to be resumed at the English School in Heliopolis, ten minutes away from Marg by car. The school had none of the charms of Leighton Park. Set in an unpicturesque desert on the outskirts of Heliopolis, it seemed to be all brick, stone, and hardened sand. However, the atmosphere was not unpleasant. I settled down to work with my usual extra math lessons and tried to make the best of it all. After two terms of satisfactory if not brilliant reports—"Doing his best," "Trying hard," "A certain amount of progress"—Miss Machray asked me if I would like to become a boarder at school. I was horrified at the thought, not that the school was so bad, but I loved living at Marg after all these years of moving around. We did not talk about it again and I took it for granted that the subject had been shelved. But at the end of the Easter holidays Aicha mentioned casually at supper that I was going back to school on Saturday. I explained that only boarders were going back on Saturday, and that I, as a day-boy, would be going back on Monday.

Then Miss Machray very calmly said: "But you are a boarder now and therefore going back on Saturday."

I was amazed and asked why this should be, since I had so clearly expressed my desire to stay at home. No explanation was forthcoming and I was told that the decision had been taken "all for my own good." Nothing I could say could draw out a better reason or change the matter.

So on Saturday I went to school as a boarder, but I was resentful: here was my reward for doing my best; very well, henceforth I would work badly and perhaps this would convince 'them' that I had better results when I was living at home. But now it was no longer going to be a matter of studies, but a question of discipline. How did I dare discuss my great-aunt's decisions? I protested my respect and affection for her (which were perfectly sincere) and said that all I wanted was to be under her roof, but my stubbornness was considered an intolerable act of insubordination.

The struggle waged on, the school authorities were consulted, end-of-term reports were bad. I was in disgrace. I had heated arguments with Miss Machray, who I think may have been more understanding than her loyalty to Great-Aunt Nimet allowed her to show. One day I was sent to call on Aunt Behidje (Princess Omar Toussoun) and what I thought was to be an ordinary visit turned out to be one long, public dressing-down, with a sermon on the evils of pride. It started with, "Il paraît que tu es orgueilleux," and it went on and on. I was completely taken back, as I had never been taxed with this supplementary sin, and I listened in humble and astonished silence while the storm raged on. And of course there was no question of allowing me a word in self-defense; one listened to one's elders but did not converse with them unless invited to. Rhetorical questions, of which there were plenty, were not to be taken advantage of.

A few days later I was back at school, but with unprecedented boldness I telephoned Marg and asked for a car to fetch me as I wanted to speak to my great-aunt. During the drive back my courage ebbed and my usual shyness got the better of me. After an hour's waiting in an anteroom I was reduced to a nervous state. When finally admitted to my great-aunt's presence, I stood mute while her wrath in no uncertain manner was unleashed upon me. Fortunately, it was mainly in Turkish, which I did not understand too well, but the tone was eloquent.

Chastised and vanquished, but unrepentant, I was driven back to school. There I decided on a plan of action. But for this I had to bide my time until I was eighteen, when, according to the law, I had the right to dispose of my person but not my inheritance. When the moment arrived, I had a final interview with one of the professors in charge of me and, seeing that nothing could be done (he sniggered, "What can you do? A palace revolution?"), I bade goodbye to my two best friends, Brian S. D. and Nevil F., and walked out defiantly by the front entrance of the school. This was against regulations—only parents and teachers were allowed that way. I took the Metro for the first time in my life and arrived in town. From there I set off on foot for Bab al-Luq Station to board a train to Ma'adi, a residential district south of Cairo, where my sister Hadidja was living.

I took her completely by surprise, still in her green satin bed, her maids drawing curtains, bringing breakfast on a tray, and without more ado I told her I had come to stay. She immediately telephoned Marg to inform them of my presence in Ma'adi. The news was very coolly received. She was told that my personal belongings would be sent over immediately, and that she herself was in disgrace, as it was obvious that she must have instigated the whole affair, since I was too much of a simpleton to take such a step by myself.

Like all family decisions of the period, these were final, dramatic, and irrevocable. Without much thought to consequences, and with all the usual ingratitude of youth to previous generations, I had crossed the Rubicon into adult life, where I was to find myself more than a little lost and bewildered. The whole world was open to me and, without knowing it, I was shedding the protection I had enjoyed since childhood. My new-found freedom was to provide me with only superficial joys and eventually to lead me into chaos.

In my new world I was to meet many delightful members of my family, some for the first time and others I had not seen for many years: Nimet and Nevine Youssry, the daughters of Princess Zeinab and Seiffoullah Youssry Pasha; their charming half-sister Loutfia, daughter of Princess Chivekiar; Zaki Halim, the son of Prince Ibrahim Halim; Prince Amr Ibrahim, reputedly the handsomest man of the family, but in my eyes especially agreeable because of his charming manners and great culture. He had three daughters, Emina, Inji, and, the eldest, the striking Nimetallah. Then there was Prince Ismail Daoud, a cavalry officer, full of fun and energy; with his monocle firmly screwed on his flushed face, he would recite in a booming voice poems in English and French as if he were giving orders for a cavalry charge. And of course our childhood playmates Saleh, Aziza, and Fayed Sabit, who were the children of my father's favorite niece, Ismet, daughter of Aunt Aziza and her husband Hassan Mohsein Pasha.

Ismet Hanem Effendi was an exceptional personality who was finally to become a national figure. On her father's side she was descended from Hassan Pasha al-Iskandarani, a naval hero of the Muhammad Ali period, and she herself manifested a keen interest in the navy. During the first Israeli war in 1948, she gave a gunboat to our naval forces. After the confiscation of our family's property in 1954, she lost all her mother's possessions, but continued with what she had left on her father's side to send bundles and packages to cadets and to keep her house open to anyone who needed help or advice. She also donated a watch to the best cadet of the year. She was greatly revered by the navy, and on her death, despite revolutionary circumstances, she was given a most solemn official funeral at which the whole naval corps turned out. She is now known to the country as Umm al-Bahriya ('the Mother of the Navy') and a charitable institution to commemorate her and bearing that name has been created. Her eldest son, Saleh, still donates a watch every year to the best cadet.

Apart from her interest in the navy, Ismet Hanem Effendi was a person of many resources and an able historian. She published in Arabic a history of the Phoenicians, and books on Ibn Battuta and Harun al-Rachid. She was compiling a monumental history of Hassan al-Iskandarani and his times when she passed away in 1973.

Renewing acquaintance with Cairo itself was also a matter of enormous excitement and interest to me. If the suburbs leading toward Marg had remained much as they had been in my childhood, the center of town had changed considerably. Formerly, it had retained many vestiges of having been a residential area. Thus the French Embassy, a fine Arab house with palm trees and yellow sand in its front courtyard, used to stand on the corner of Sherif and Qasr al-Nil Streets; now, a huge block of flats had gone up, with shops on the street level. The street itself had been broadened at the expense of the trees on the sidewalks. Commerce had taken precedence over leisure.

Similarly, in Soliman Pasha Street, the villas that had stood there had shared the fate of the French Embassy and had been replaced by blocks of flats and several cinemas. In Garden City, the area's most beautiful house, which had been situated on the Nile between the Semiramis Hotel and the British Embassy, had been demolished. It had been the Khediva Mother's white palace, with avenues of yellow sand and green lawns studded with white royal palms. Its gateway of marble and black-and-gilded ironwork, surmounted by a crown, gave on Qasr al-Dubara Square. It had been a colorful entrance to the district with its porters and attendants dressed in Oriental costumes. Today the gateway, minus its crown, can be seen at the government-owned villa of Prince Abd al-Munim in Heliopolis.

Apart from the intrinsic charm of the place, its destruction was a pity, since its owner had probably been the most loved of the reigning ladies of Egypt. The Khediva Mother was born the Princess Emina, daughter of Prince Ilhamy, the son of Abbas I, and was the wife of the Khedive Tewfik. In possession of a large personal fortune, she gave a great part of it away in donations and charitable institutions, and was surnamed Umm al-Muhsinin, 'the Mother of Charity.' A girls' school that she founded, whose principal ornament is a heavy, ornate *sabil* in Turkish baroque style, stands close to the mosque of Ibn Tulun. It is now known by the name of Umm Abbas, 'Mother of Abbas.' It is a way of making the donor as anonymous as possible, since the ignorant passerby cannot possibly be expected to know that the 'Abbas' referred to is the Khedive Abbas Hilmy II.

Princess Emina was as beautiful as she was kind and dignified, and in her person she defies all laws of heredity, for her grandfather, Abbas I (r.1848–54), is usually considered the most critical ruler of our family. Abbas was the grandson of Muhammad Ali and the son of Toussoun. His grandfather allowed him to be brought up by his grandmother, Emina of Nosratli, as a consolation for the loss of her two sons: Toussoun, who died at an early age, and Ismail, burnt alive in the Sudan. Emina lavished all her frustrated love on her grandson, and although Muhammad Ali saw that the child was being spoiled he did not have the heart to interfere. Intelligent and courageous as he was seen to be during the Syrian campaign, Abbas could not bear any form of discipline and particularly resented his uncle Ibrahim Pasha's continuous call to order as well as his fame. When Abbas reached the throne, he opposed all that had been done in the previous reign. He persecuted cabinet ministers and even his own family, who fled in all directions, some retiring to their estates and others seeking asylum in Istanbul.

He was opposed to modern progress and put a stop to institutions and projects designed to 'westernize' the country—a popular move, since the masses did not appreciate having to undergo a continuous, forced, evolution foreign to their habits. They quite naturally preferred to sink back into the traditional culture to which they were accustomed. This was to make him one of Egypt's most popular rulers, if not the best. Although anti-European by instinct, he was completely tolerant in religious matters and protected all faiths in his dominions. During the Crimean war, a *firman* arrived from Istanbul, ordering the expulsion of the Greek community from Egypt. Abbas delayed the execution of this edict until a solution had been found by having the American Consul-General in Egypt take the Greek community under his protection. When reproved for not having acted more severely, Abbas shrugged away the matter and answered that since the Greeks were living under the protection of the American flag, he did not wish to insult that great nation by molesting them.

Continuing his contrary attitude to the previous reign, Abbas gave preference to British technicians over French, and it was they who built the first railway line, thus getting Abbas a bad press from the French. Agriculture continued to prosper, but not industry. His great passion was for horses, and he had splendid stud farms that greatly improved horse-breeding in the country. And finally it must be said to his credit that he left the country solvent and with no public debt.

By some Abbas was described as an old-fashioned Turkish gentleman with exquisite manners; others just saw in him a somber despot. (Why can't a despot have beautiful manners, I wonder?) He would at times seclude himself in desert palaces, from which rumors of strange rites began to be whispered. Nothing is known for certain of accusations of dissipation held against him, accusations which may well have been inaccurate or exaggerated as they so often are when a person holds high office, but his death seems to confirm his bad reputation. He was murdered in his palace of Benha by two male slaves.

The two men disappeared into the night and were never heard of again. No reason was ever found for the crime, but one of the theories is that Abbas had threatened them with execution for some fault they had committed, and to save their own necks they had murdered him. This does not make sense, for they then would have been under arrest or at any rate have had no access to his person. The second theory is that they had been sent to him for that purpose by one of his kinswomen in Istanbul, but no name has ever been put forward. The only thing that is certain is that the crime was not committed for political reasons, but was of a personal nature.

The Governor of Cairo, Elfi Bey, on hearing the news, had the corpse dressed and put in a carriage on a seat next to himself. Surrounded by the magnificent household cavalry, they drove back to Cairo to one of the palaces at the Citadel and there the governor, pointing his guns on the city, tried to have Abbas's son, Ilhami, proclaimed ruler of Egypt instead of Said, the natural heir. But the plot failed and Said ascended the throne. Ilhami married a Turkish Imperial Sultana and proceeded to lead a leisurely existence in Turkey. He died there when his boat capsized on the Bosphorous and he was swept away by a strong current.

As in Turkey, the reins of government in Egypt were inherited by the eldest member of the family and this would not necessarily be the sovereign's son. Abbas had tried to change the law in favor of his son, bypassing Said and eventually Ibrahim Pasha's children. He tried to discredit the latter by spreading a rumor that Ibrahim had not been Muhammad Ali's son at all, but was the son of Emina of Nosratli by a previous marriage to her tutor. This brainwave had been the idea of Ilhami's own tutor, a certain Lala Ali Pasha. Unfortunately, for more reasons than one, it did not bear any close examination.

Emina was married to her tutor as a child of ten so that he could be sure to control her fortune. The marriage was never consummated and he died, leaving her free to a real marriage with Muhammad Ali. What Lala Ali Pasha casually overlooked was that the first child of Emina and Muhammad Ali was not Ibrahim but the very famous Princess Tawhida, whose identity as Muhammad Ali's daughter nobody—not even Abbas— had contested. She was famous not only for her personal merits but because she simply happened to be her father's favorite child. She is referred to in the documents of the day, rather embarrassingly, as "the fruit of Emina's virginity."

Pat Campell, a representative of the British government, had questioned Muhammad Ali on his first children and he had answered: "I had five children by my first wife; they were all born at Cavalla. My first child was a girl (Tawhida), who married Muharram Bey,[1] then followed Ibrahim, Toussoun, and Ismail, and the last was Nazli, who married the Defterdar of Egypt. Of all my children, Ibrahim was the only one to be nurtured by his mother. There was an epidemic of plague when he was born in Cavalla and his mother preferred to look after her first boy herself."

When Ibrahim was sixteen years old, the Sultan demanded him as a hostage and a guarantee of Muhammad Ali's loyalty. During this period it is said that he was replaced in his father's affections by his younger brother, Toussoun, who was so charming that he was always referred to as 'the Charming Toussoun.' But when Ibrahim was allowed to return to Egypt, he soon regained his father's esteem and affection. They were finally to collaborate so closely that one can say that the last part of Muhammad Ali's reign was partly Ibrahim's.

Ibrahim's son, the Khedive Ismail, was to succeed where Abbas had failed and to change officially the law of inheritance of the throne from father to son. This was accomplished through legal proceedings endorsed by the Sublime Porte—the supreme authority in all civil and religious matters. Understandably, this act aroused the fury of some (not all) branches of the family, who would now not ever see the throne revert to them; and so the old story about Ibrahim Pasha was brought out of its moth balls (as it still is today when convenient!). Two princes went further and actually plotted to overthrow Ismail, but the conspiracy was averted. The two subversive plotters were asked to leave the country and were allowed to take their enormous fortunes with them. They did so and settled down in Turkey. (One of the princes took out four million gold pounds, an enormous sum for the period. At his death his children were to find themselves completely ruined by their father's extravagance; they were invited back to Egypt by the Khedive Ismail, who provided handsomely for them.)

Abbas left his name to a flourishing residential district, but Abbasiya is also one of the main military sites of Cairo. As it is close to the desert, camps and barracks can extend in that direction almost indefinitely, and

---

[1] The district in Alexandria in which they lived is still called by their name, 'Muharram Bey,' just as 'Mustafa Pasha' is where Prince Mustafa Fazil had a summer residence for his harem by the sea.

have in fact been doing so up to the present day. The residential part of the district has gone down in the world, with only a few of its genteel landmarks—in the form of some large villas—still in evidence. These are in a dilapidated state, but display interesting architectural details, basically European features intermingling with some oriental latticework reminiscent of the mashrabiya used for harems.

One of the characteristics of Cairene residential districts is that they never remain for long in fashion, with the result that few families can claim to have lived for more than two generations in the same house. People seem to move to newer districts, discarding their previous home without, one feels, even a parting glance over their shoulders. In this manner Shubra has changed completely in character. Its famous avenue of sycamore trees leading to Muhammad Ali's palace, its lavish mansions with gardens overflowing with shrubs and trees, have become a slum. The trees of the avenue have been cut down, and in the place of elegant carriages and cavaliers, a proletarian tram goes clanging down its main street.

Garden City, the most chic of all these districts, originated as Cairo's dumping place for refuse. Ibrahim Pasha had the mounds leveled and planted orange groves on the site, and for decades it was known as 'Ibrahim Pasha's plantations.' Then he built a palace for himself (not luxurious but spacious), the Palace of Qasr al-Dubara, and, farther south, another one (sumptuous), Saraya al-Kubra, for his wife Hoshiar. The property was split up by their heirs and descendants and finally passed into the public sector, when it was named Garden City by the English company that acquired it in 1906.

The road that follows along the Nile was blocked at the British Embassy, which allowed itself the unique privilege of having its garden reach the river. All other houses had had their gardens curtailed to let the road pass by, including the great houses on the opposite Giza shore. So the British Embassy remained in isolated splendor until 1952 and the final British withdrawal from Egypt. The situation was then rectified, and now the Corniche al-Nil follows the Nile without any interruption.

In the 1920s Adly Pasha Yeghen's daughter, Neila Hanum, built a fine palace,[1] also on the Corniche al-Nil, which gave the district great distinc-

---

[1] The architect was Lasciac Bey.

tion.Unfortunately this too has been demolished, and even people usually indifferent to such goings-on murmured their disapproval at seeing it destroyed. The interior was beautifully decorated; I remember in particular one room where there was a fine collection of Islamic books and calligraphy, and also a very pretty dining room in Wedgwood green with white stucco work. The Yeghen family are descendants of Muhammad Ali's sister Zibenda Kadin. Muhammad Ali bestowed the name Yeghen on his sister's children, the word in Turkish meaning nephews.

Today Garden City is no longer what it used to be. Athough there are some villas left, and several embassies have independent houses and gardens, many commercial firms have opened up premises in the district. The resulting increase in noisy traffic jams along its narrow streets, which follow the paths of the Qasr al-Ali gardens, makes Garden City very similar to the business center of town. But every now and again one comes across some old fruit trees that remind one of Ibrahim Pasha's plantations, and some of the streets have kept names that are evocative of the past such Saraya al-Kubra, or al-Salamlik Street, where the author lives in a very modest flat.

Cairo in the 1940s, like any pleasant capital, had numerous foreign colonies. Many had been there for generations and had become very much part of the country. They were a great asset, for they brought with them their own national skills, skills that were often lacking in Egypt, and in this manner we had our foreign experts already at hand. It would be both unrealistic and ungrateful to deny all that we owe to them. They undoubtedly profited from the country, but the country just as surely benefited from them.

Many celebrities were to be found in all sorts of intellectual fields. Among these I was privileged to come into contact with a person whose personal merits remain for me a wonder of human realization. Ignace Tiegerman, I write his name with music in my ears, was of poor health, and because of this and his fondness for the country, he settled down in Cairo, where, with other gifted musicians, he created a musical academy, the Conservatoire Tiegerman. A small, frail man with an astonishing resemblance to Horowitz, he had an indomitable spirit and enormous pride and dignity. It was extraordinary to hear all the different emotions that came pouring out of his superb piano-playing, emotions that were nevertheless always tempered by his perfect sense of style and taste.

In everyday life he showed the same critical judgment in the choice of an oriental prayer rug, an early painting by Macrese, or an old Arab chest. He would sometimes invite me to share his lunch, and by adding something quite simple to a very ordinary dish he would turn it into a new and interesting piece of cuisine. His sense of humor was always present, mordant, sardonic, but also delightful. Once when I had played a rather tricky passage of Chopin's to his liking, he turned to me and said: "Vous avez joué ça comme le fils naturel de Cortot!" Real compliments were few and far between, and his temper when roused was equally memorable and scathing; he was renowned for it and everybody stood a bit in awe of him. One day when I arrived obviously unprepared for a lesson, he just said quite loudly, as if talking to himself: "Really I am a most unfortunate person never to have had a gifted pupil!" I think music to him was sacred and to arrive unprepared at a lesson was admitting a kind of lack of faith.

He died in Cairo of a painful illness that he bore with fortitude, but it was pitiful to watch that already frail body shrink on the last day to almost the size of a child's. To those that knew him he has become something of a cult, and when they meet they feel a bond in common like people who have undergone a great experience together.

There were innumerable musical events in Cairo, recitals, ballets, operas, and an excellent symphony orchestra under the direction of the Austrian maestro Franz Lichauer. I can bring to mind memorable performances of Brahms, Rachmaninoff, and Chopin concertos with Tiegerman at the piano. Tiegerman had the wonderful gift of sweeping through the movements of each work and creating a symphonic whole that left one breathless.

Most of the important activities that needed a stage were held at Cairo's Opera House, built by Avoscani and Rossi. Many buildings had changed on my return to Cairo, but the Opera House had remained much the same as when it had been built for the inauguration of the Suez Canal, except that when gas light had been replaced by electricity a great chandelier in the center of the house had been replaced by a crystal plafonnière. There one could see *Aida* in its original costumes and sets. It had been commissioned by the Khedive Ismail for the opening night, but as it was not finished in time, *Rigoletto* was given in its stead. The Khedive kept in constant touch with Verdi and collaborated to some extent with the libretto. This is seen by some as evidence of his already aroused interest in Ethiopia, with the military campaign that was to follow.

The Opera House was quite small but well built, with a deep stage which performers appreciated but which also contributed to the cold draughts sometimes felt in front rows. The decoration was all in a traditional white and gold and red plush, a delightful background to set off the elegance of a glittering audience. Cairo glittered in those days; it could muster up an extraordinarily decorative assembly of attractive and elegant women of foreign or Egyptian nationalities.

In our own family, the reigning beauties were the Princess Fawzia (at the time Empress of Iran) and her sister the Princess Faiza, King Farouk's sisters. Also three other sisters, Turkish imperial princesses, the Sultanas Neslishah, Hanzadé, and Heybetullah, married to three Egyptian princes: Princes Abdel Munim, Muhammad Ali Ibrahim, and Amr Ibrahim. And the wives of Princes Said and Hassan Toussoun, the Princesses Mahivech and Fatma. I remember quite well the first time I saw Princess Neslishah. I had just arrived from England and she, newly married, had come to lunch at Marg. For most of the meal I remained gaping at her in open-mouthed admiration, but I think my loutishness may be excused, as I was facing for the first time what surely must have been one of the great beauties of our time.

Discussions were endless as to who should be considered the loveliest of these ladies, but I think for the main public and the country in general it was Princess Fawzia, with her classical, photogenic features, who became the symbol of legendary beauty. Cecil Beaton wrote this description of her when he saw her in Iran:

"If ever Botticelli were reincarnated and wished to paint an Asiatic Venus or Primavera, here is his subject. He would delight in the Queen's features, contained in the perfect heart-shaped face, the strangely pale but piercing blue eyes, the crimson-coloured lips, curling like wrought-iron volutes, and the way in which the dark-chestnut hair grows so beautifully from the forehead."[1]

On the other hand, I was once admiring some of the above-mentioned ladies at a dinner party at the Turkish Embassy in honor of the Vilaverdes.[2] I was speaking about them with the wife of the Spanish

---

[1] Cecil Beaton, *Near East*. London: Batsford, 1943.
[2] The Marchesa de Vilaverde was General Franco's daughter.

ambassador, Madame de los Barcenas, but she waved everything aside with an energetic: "Oui, oui, mais la seule c'est Faiza." And this too was and still is the opinion of many people who have had the privilege of knowing that charming princess.

Unfortunately there is no portrait that does her justice and in photographs she hardly ever comes out well. But more than her beauty and grace and naturally controlled low speaking voice, her kindness, simplicity, and charm made her a quite exceptional figure. She had a way of listening patiently to the most pedantic people as if they were the most interesting persons on earth, which would make them leave her presence elated and their footsteps lighter than they had been before. She moved with a slow tempo of her own and I have never seen her flustered or giving any sign of being hurried in any circumstances.

There are innumerable incidents that I can recollect about her, but I shall just put down one tiny but rather sad one, since it occurred just before she was to leave Egypt forever. It was some time after the 1952 revolution. We were driving in her car, she seated in front by the window and I in the middle between her and the chauffeur, with her husband Bülent and a couple of friends in the back seat, when we were stopped by a traffic jam near the Qasr al-Nil bridge. A group of young schoolgirls, dressed in their uniforms, spotted her and came running across the traffic like a flock of birds, and said to her: "Faiza, Faiza, do not worry, whatever may happen you will always be our princess."

The Opera House unfortunately is no more. It was burned down in 1971 with all its historic treasures. It is generally accepted, though not officially so, that it was arson. It has left a great gap in one of Cairo's main squares, and Ibrahim Pasha's equestrian statue looks a bit forlorn without the Opera's architectural background. Once before, this statue had been the victim of violence when the rebel Urabi had it dismantled; but not for long, for when that gentleman had fled at the first sound of cannon from the battlefield of Tell al-Kabir (it takes more than just being a rebel to be a hero!) and thrown himself on the mercy of the Khedive Tewfik, the statue of Egypt's greatest soldier was reinstated in its present place.

Ibrahim Pasha (1789–1848) is one of the most inspiring figures of his times and he was to strike the imagination of many of his contemporaries. Physically, his resemblance to his father, the great Muhammad Ali, was quite apparent. They were both short but powerfully built men with, in the case of Ibrahim Pasha, rather short arms. Ibrahim had a much more oval face than Muhammad Ali, but the family resemblance between the two men was unmistakable.

Of a jovial nature, Ibrahim was highly emotional, as was seen when he was forced to disband his Syrian regiments; his parting speech had all the soldiers in tears and embracing each other. "He was a good friend and equally good hater, though not vindictive or cruel."[1] He was worshipped by his troops, to whom he was always an example, sharing their hardships, sleeping on the ground, joining and sitting down with them at meal times. He would make the rounds after a battle and help the doctors with the wounded. And the incredible impetuosity with which he would charge or pursue the enemy could not but be contagious.

A French poet wrote of him, "L'occident n'a pas vu de soldat plus intrépide, plus généreux, plus né pour la victoire . . . . Ouvrez lui le monde, il ira jusqu'au bout. Il est de la race de ces hommes qui ne s'arrêtent que lorsqu'ils tombent, comme Alexandre ou Gengis Khan."[2] Lamartine agrees with this point of view and says that Ibrahim can only be compared with Alexander the Great as a hero.

In his first major campaign—in 1816, at the age of 27, in central Arabia— Ibrahim was to attain the highest honors within the Ottoman empire. The Wahhabis, an extremely austere Muslim sect, had taken Mecca and the Holy Places and destroyed the accumulated treasures of centuries. In an earlier military expedition, Muhammad Ali had regained power over the holy cities of Mecca and Medina, but the Wahhabis were in control of the interior. Muhammad Ali decided to give the command of this second expedition to his son Ibrahim. It was to be a most grueling campaign, fought through desert sand and scorching sun until the army finally reached Derayeh, the Wahhabite capital, which was surrounded by a series of forts. The Egyptian army at times lacked both food and ammu-

---

[1] De Leon, *The Khedive's Egypt.*
[2] Général Weygand, *L'Histoire militaire de Mohamed Ali et ses fils.*

nition and was suffering from many ailments including dysentery. Ibrahim, along with his men, suffered enormously, and there were moments when it looked as if he and his soldiers would perish from sheer exhaustion. But Ibrahim possessed all the qualities needed to wrench a victory from such a situation, and he conquered Derayeh and the whole of the Nejd.

The Wahhabite leaders were taken to Cairo, where they were treated honorably. But the Sublime Porte asked for them to be sent to Istanbul, and there they were tortured and executed. Ibrahim Pasha withheld one child that he did not have the heart to send to certain death. But the Ottomans demanded him too. Ibrahim in answer sent them a letter which is now in the King Faysal Institute in Riyadh.[1] It contained the names of all his children, among them that of the young Wahhabite prince, Abd al-Wahab. Ibrahim told the Ottoman authorities to choose any name on the list. They did not dare name anyone who was considered part of Ibrahim's family, and in this manner the young Abd al-Wahab was saved.

After this campaign Ibrahim's fame was instantaneous, for now all devout Muslims could resume the pilgrimage to Mecca. For this he was made Pasha of the Holy Places, a title that gave him precedence over all the pashas of the Ottoman empire, including his father. This was clearly a trick to try to antagonize father and son, but to no avail; Muhammad Ali was furious at the shabby slight and it merely confirmed his suspicion of Ottoman bad faith toward him.

Ibrahim's next military assignment took him to Europe, when in 1824 the Sultan of Turkey, unable to control the Greek insurgents fighting for their freedom in the Peloponnesus, was once again obliged to ask Muhammad Ali's help. (This reminds one of Nicholas I of Russia being asked by the Emperor of Austria to come and quell a Hungarian revolt, which 'the Policeman of Europe' obligingly did.) Muhammad Ali sent Ibrahim to pacify the Peloponnesus. In four months he took the city of Missolonghi, which had for years resisted the Ottoman General Rashid Pasha.

But from then on, Muhammad Ali and Ibrahim Pasha were to break from Istanbul and find themselves in open conflict with Turkey. It had been understood that, as a reward for success in the Peloponnesian cam-

---

[1] This information was given to me by the Turkish diplomat Hüsnü Kurhan.

paign, they would receive the pashaliks of Palestine and Syria, territories that were essential to Egyptian ambitions. But this did not happen. Instead, the Sultan gave Muhammad Ali the island of Pathos, opposite Cavalla, as a personal hereditary possession, and the pashaliks of Candia (Crete) and Cyprus, which were of absolutely no strategic interest to him.

After the relationship between Istanbul and Egypt had deteriorated to the point of open acts of hostility on the Turkish side, Ibrahim marched into Palestine (1831), where his first victory was the taking of Acre, considered invulnerable after its successful resistance to Napoleon. From there on, history records a series of successes that read like a geographical progression heading north toward the Turkish border. Ibrahim made a triumphant entry into Damascus and Jerusalem, where he re-established the rights of the Christian minorities and pilgrims. This was followed by an important battle at Homs, after which Syria was completely taken over. On the Turkish frontier, a battle was fought at Beïian, allowing the Egyptian army to march beyond the Taurus into Asia Minor as far as Konya. Here there took place a decisive battle that left the Turkish capital open to Ibrahim Pasha. The situation then took on an international dimension, since the European powers suddenly saw their Middle Eastern policy at risk if the Ottoman empire were allowed to collapse. Muhammad Ali was prevailed upon to return to within the frontiers of Syria, but he insisted on keeping Adana and the control of the Taurus mountain passes. At this point, his empire extended, apart from Egypt, over Arabia and the Hedjaz, Nubia and the Sudan, Syria, Palestine, Lebanon, and the region of Adana. Pat Campbell writes in 1834: "He is *de jure* a vassal and *de facto* he is independent."

The European powers kept harassing Muhammad Ali as they held to their policy of preserving the tottering Turkish empire at the expense of Egypt. He made some minor concessions but refused to reduce the size of the army, which was the main European objective. Unfortunately for Egypt and the Middle East as a whole, a strong power in the Orient was contrary to European political aims.

While Europe and Russia were badgering Muhammad Ali, the Turks were rearming. Muhammad Ali gave Ibrahim instructions never to cross the frontiers set after the Battle of Konya, thus keeping to the letter of his word not only toward the Sultan but also to the ever-vigilant European powers, which, as usual, were working against him. Lord Ponsonby, the

British ambassador to Istanbul, incited the Sultan to attack Ibrahim again, and he himself had agents in Syria (among them Lady Stanhope), who tried to provoke revolt against the Egyptian administration. The situation became tense as continual frontier incidents were started by the Turkish Generalissimo. Ibrahim Pasha writes to him a most revealing letter:[1]

"You have crossed our frontiers, you have attacked villages under our jurisdiction, you have fired on our military outposts. Is it by order of the Sultan? I must report to my father of these doings. Are you acting as a provincial governor or as a military chief? I summon you to explain your behavior, which nothing we have done could have warranted. We have respected the frontiers of your governorship, and you will never find us in an illegal position.

"I prefer to think, General, that you have not been trying to intimidate me, and that these events are a misunderstanding which could turn out to be a disaster to Islam. Such acts are particularly reprehensible, as war is not conducive toward the civilization which our master the Sultan is striving for in Turkey or *His Highness my father in the Arab world*. War, which is of no profit to anyone, victimizes the civilian populations and can only be a hindrance to all progress. Solidarity, peace, work are the only means by which we can strive to attain that which our ancestors had reached."

This letter unveils Muhammad Ali's vision of the Sultan governing the Turkish-speaking states and the Balkans, and himself creating a pan-Arab state ruled from Cairo. The resurrection of a United Arab Nation was certainly one of the chief reasons for Europe's unrelenting opposition to Muhammad Ali. His intentions must have been quite clear in his day, although now there is a wish to discredit this theory. However, Lord Palmerston wrote at the time: "His real design is to establish an Arabian Kingdom, including all the countries of which Arabic is the language." And Professor Dodwell: "Indeed, could Muhammad Ali have asserted his independence, the Egyptian Caliphate would certainly have been revived."[2] Lamartine likewise mentions Muhammad Ali's plans for an Arab empire in a preface to the works of Estournel on Turkey, published in 1846.

---

[1] Dodwell, *The Founder of Modern Egypt*. Emphasis mine.
[2] Ibid.

Egyptian hereditary independence was to be achieved, but this time Europe was to throw all pretenses to the wind and go up in arms against Muhammad Ali. Turkey attacked the first Egyptian outposts, who drew back in face of the vastly superior numbers of the Turkish army. But finally, on June 29, 1839, the 70,000 Turks and the 30,000 Egyptians[55] met at Nezib, where the Turks were overwhelmingly defeated. The Turkish commander-in-chief, Hafiz Pasha (also surrounded by a group of Prussian officers led by General von Moltke), fled, leaving everything to the enemy, including his luxurious tent (described as "a vast palace and furnished as luxuriously as an emperor's reception room"), his cannons and armaments, and finally his papers and dispatches. Hafiz was a young favorite of Sultan Mahmud's; he fought courageously but was not an able tactician.

The battle of Nezib was the most complete of victories. The prestige of Muhammad Ali and his son was at its highest point, and everybody saw in them the potential saviors of the Turkish empire under a new leadership. In July, the whole of the Turkish Ottoman fleet, under the command of its admiral, the Captain-Pasha Ahmed Fawza, left Istanbul and gave itself up to Muhammad Ali in Alexandria—the Captain-Pasha declaring that Muhammad Ali was the only man worthy of wielding the scepter of the Turkish empire and being its padishah. Turkey was quick to open negotiations with Muhammad Ali before things got any worse. Egypt became the hereditary possession of Muhammad Ali and his descendants. Most of his other demands were also accepted.

Events moved so fast that Europe was taken by surprise, except for France, which even before Nezib had put pressure on Muhammad Ali not to move on to the Turkish capital. As Muhammad Ali put it, it had been "a family affair" within the frontiers of the Ottoman empire. Now France, under the premiership of Marshal Soult, was the first to affirm Europe's right to participate in any matter concerning 'l'affaire d'Orient.' Accordingly, it sent a note, together with the governments of Russia, Austria, Britain, and Prussia, to the Sublime Port, saying that the Europen powers did not recognize the Turco-Egyptian agreement, and that all such pacts must first pass through the chancelleries of the five European coun-

---

[55] These figures are stated in a letter from Ibrahim Pasha to his father.

tries. As French Admiral Roussin is reputed to have said to the French Consul-General, Cochelet, in Alexandria: "Muhammad Ali must be made to understand that since the five principal European powers have come to an agreement, *they will decide the Middle East situation in a manner favorable to European interest.*" Thus what normally would have been considered an outrageous intervention in Turkish national affairs was received by the Sultan with incredulous delight, for he now no longer had to face Muhammad Ali by himself.

The most complex diplomatic haggling and intrigues were to ensue, laying bare all the ambitions of the five European powers. The tale makes very good reading and one can follow the thread that leads to the First World War. But eventually the victim was to be Egypt. France, the instigator of 'l'affaire d'Orient,' had a new government, dissociated itself from the 'five' when they took up arms against Muhammad Ali, and even went so far as to plead his cause. But Palmerston was adamant and decided to crush Muhammad Ali, even out of Egypt.

The very fact that Muhammad Ali was on good terms with France (there was a new administration, and French public opinion, as we shall see, was very much in his favor) made him suspect as regards British interests in the Mediterranean. Pressures of all sorts were brought to bear on him, ranging from negotiations (always to his disadvantage) to military threats of bombarding Alexandria. Finally, Sir Charles Napier, who was in charge of a joint Anglo-Turco-Austro-Prussian and Russian force, attacked Ibrahim Pasha in Syria. He bombarded, indiscriminately, military targets and defenseless villages and towns on the coast of Syria and Palestine;[1] in 1840 Beirut was completely destroyed and went down in flames. Rather than see the same fate overtake Alexandria, Muhammad Ali recalled Ibrahim from Syria, from where he made a difficult retreat back to Egypt. The Egyptian army was disbanded on the demand of the European powers, and all that was left of the Egyptian empire was the Sudan. But Alexandria had been saved from holocaust, and Egypt remained the hereditary possession of Muhammad Ali and his house. The Turkish navy was returned to Turkey.

The toils of war had taken a heavy toll on Ibrahim's health. His most

---

[1] Aimé Vingtrinier, *Soliman-Pacha: Generalissime des armées égyptiennes,* Paris, 1886.

testing campaign was in 1821, when he led the Egyptian expeditionary force in search of the sources of the Nile. On the way up the White Nile, he was taken violently ill with dysentery, and suffered loss of blood, a high fever, and racking head pains. Unable to march or ride any more, he continued prostrate, either by water or in a litter carried between two camels. His doctors (all Italians; one died on the way) tried to dissuade him from continuing any farther. But he insisted on carrying on until another doctor, sent to him by Muhammad Ali, told him quite bluntly that if he persisted in his aim he would not answer for his life. He then agreed to be taken back by boat to Egypt, where he landed at one of his palaces on the island of Roda. This palace was relatively small in comparison with most Cairene palaces; it had only a small retinue of servants, but it had a very fine collection of antiques, Egyptian, Greek, and Islamic, which was partly to form our first museum. The southern part of the island, where the Nilometer is situated, belonged to the Monasterli family; the central part to the Sherif family; and we must suppose that Ibrahim's own house stood on the site of the present Palace of Manial. Muhammad Ali joined him there and did not leave his bedside for three months until there were definite signs of his recovery. All the doctors agreed that if it had not been for Ibrahim Pasha's remarkable constitution he would never have been well again.

In 1845 Ibrahim was again taken seriously ill from the consequences of the Nilotic campaign. He was advised to go to Italy and to take the waters at San Guitano, near Pisa. There the Grand Duke of Tuscany received him warmly and put a wing of his own palace at his disposal. Ibrahim visited Florence, where splendid receptions were given in his honor. From then on, his whole trip was to change in character and instead of being just a private journey his tour became a manifestation of his popularity, and of international recognition of his military achievements, although inevitably, of course, his father's name was associated with his.

The waters of San Guitano did not turn out to be beneficial, and Ibrahim decided to seek the help of French doctors. At Genoa he boarded the Egyptian frigate *The Nile* and reached the French naval base of Toulon, where the admiral ship of the French navy, together with a fort on land, fired a 21-gun salute. The Egyptian frigate answered the compliment. Any further pretense at traveling incognito was at this point clearly impossible, and Ibrahim Pasha, wearing his magnificent golden parade uniform constellated with diamond decorations and followed by his civilian and military suite, landed at Toulon. The whole population of the city gave to the Egyptian hero what was said to have been a delirious welcome.

He was greeted with the same enthusiasm when he reached Marseilles, where the French government had prepared a house for him. But he preferred to stay with the Pastré family, wealthy bourgeois merchants who had longstanding ties with Egypt. Standing on the doorstep of the villa, the head of the family, the old grandmother, surrounded by all her relatives, presented the keys of the house to Ibrahim Pasha with the words: "Henceforth this house belongs to Your Highness."

Ibrahim's reception at Marseilles moved him deeply and he found it hard to leave that generous city, but his doctors were worried for his health and prevailed upon him to move on, for a cure, to Vernet in the Pyrenees. A Colonel Thierry was detached by the French government to accompany him there. The little city welcomed him with the usual military honors, and a triumphal arch was raised, bearing the inscription: "Au vainqueur de Konya et de Nézib." This was followed by a second arch, this time with a more elaborate inscription:

> *Au digne fils de Méhmét Ali,*
> *Au civilisateur de l'Orient,*
> *A l'ami des Français,*
> *Au héros égyptien.*

At Vernet he followed a strict and uninterrupted course of medical treatment for five months, at the end of which Dr. Lallemand joyfully announced that his patient was completely cured. This was to be only partially the case, as Ibrahim Pasha's health was never to be good again, though five months of mountain air must certainly have been a wonderful antidote to the African Nilotic climate. The truth was that he was a dying man, and in the portraits of the period he looks as old as his father, although to the end he maintained an upright military carriage and an alert soldier's eye, while the sound of his boots could be heard from afar shaking the parquet floors of Ras al-Tin as he entered that palace.

The French capital now awaited Ibrahim Pasha. King Louis-Philippe received him magnificently; the Elysée Palace, then known as the Bourbon-Elysée, was put at his disposal, and as a special compliment the rooms used by Napoleon were prepared for his personal use. The King's son, the Duc de Montpensier, was charged by his father to be his escort during his stay in the capital. A great military parade was staged, at which Ibrahim Pasha took the salute on horseback. In further honor of his visit, the mint struck a commemorative medallion bearing a portrait of Muhammad Ali and the inscription: "Méhmét Ali, régénérateur de l'Egypte." And finally the King bestowed on him the Grand Cordon of the Légion d'Honneur.

Everywhere that he had gone, friendly, curious crowds had gathered, and this was also to be true when, after some deliberation, he extended his tour to England. There Queen Victoria was at her most gracious during his audience, ordering that all his wishes should be seen to and, at the moment of his departure from the country, inquiring if everything had gone satisfactorily and all had been done to make his stay agreeable. Ibrahim's main interest in England had been touring the industrial cities to keep abreast with the latest scientific research in order to bring back to Egypt any innovation that could be useful to the country. But of course there had been many social occasions as well, and when he had encountered the Duke of Wellington it was said "that the greatest soldier of the East had met the greatest soldier of the West."

Ibrahim Pasha was to die in Egypt a few months before his father, and since no tomb had been prepared for him, he was placed in the one that had been made ready for Muhammad Ali at one of the family cemeteries near the Imam al-Shafei mausoleum. To spare the sick and ailing father, then at Shubra, the shock of his son's death, the news was withheld from him. But in his last years of senility Muhammad Ali was credited with astonishing flashes of second sight, and it is said that at the exact moment they were lowering Ibrahim into his grave, Muhammad Ali suddenly looked up and said: "They are burying Ibrahim. Now Abbas will reign and all our work will be undone."

But to this day the peasants of southern Turkey remember Ibrahim Pasha in their evening prayers for his enlightened administration there. "Akşama hürmet, sabaha niyet, kolumuza kuvvet, Agamiza beret, hükümetize nusret, kesemize bereket, Ibrahim Paşa'ya rahmet, peygamberize salavat."

As we see, this prayer rhymes in Turkish. Roughly translated, the meaning without rhyme goes: "Respects to the evening, project for the morning, strength to our arms, prosperity for our Aga, allegiance to our government, prosperity for our finances, blessings on the soul of Ibrahim Pasha, prayers to the Prophet."

Almost a century after the Turco-Egyptian wars, Egypt was at peace and watched as a spectator while the rest of the world was at war. During the Second World War, Egypt was officially a neutral country, but was in fact much more involved than such a position would warrant. It was the most important British base in the Near East, and on my arrival from England I found Cairo in a fantastic turmoil, playing host to all sorts of armies: English, Australian, New Zealander, South African, Polish, Greek, Yugoslav, and others.

Among Egyptians, feelings were divided about the war. Some were for the Allies because of their way of life, and others were pro-Axis because they were the enemies of the British; among these latter, expectations were running high. But others were pro-German because they had had educational links with that country or were simply admirers of German force, organization, and methods without looking too deeply beyond that.

In internal affairs the political party that dominated all others was the Wafd. Its leader was Mustafa al-Nahhas Pasha, a man of humble origins who by his personal talents and magnetism had reached this eminent position. The Wafd had changed considerably from its beginnings when, under the leadership of Saad Zaghloul, my father had participated so wholeheartedly in its midst. At Saad Pasha's death differences had arisen within its ranks, and splinter parties had been formed. The new leaders of the Wafd were a very different lot, and were credited with a personally ambitious policy of undermining the monarchy and forming a republic, which they thought would automatically come under their sway.

Of course a patriotic anti-British attitude was the official stand, and yet the Wafd agreed to come to power with the aid of British guns and bayonets. The situation reached crisis point in 1942. On February 4, the British ambassador, Sir Miles Lampson (later known as Lord Killearn), trying to force a change of government to which King Farouk was opposed, proceeded to surround the Palace of Abdeen with tanks; road blocks were set up at all issues from Abbasiya, where the Egyptian army was stationed. Flanked by two armed A.D.C.s, Lampson moved into the Palace, where

Teymour Pasha, one of the chamberlains, wanted to precede the invading party to announce them to the King, but Lampson, a big burly man, brushed him aside with an "I know my way." Arriving at the door to the King's study, Lampson was stopped by Hassanein Pasha, who pointed out that no one carrying arms was allowed into the King's presence. Lampson agreed to leave the two A.D.C.s in the anteroom with Hassanein while he himself was introduced into the King's study. There he presented the young monarch with an abdication paper to sign, after which he would be deported to either Cyprus or Ceylon.

The document had been prepared by Sir Walter Monckton, who happened to be passing through Egypt at the time and had previously supervised the abdication papers of Edward VIII. Embossed on the Egyptian document were the words "British Embassy," a final humiliation. The King took a look at the paper, and commented wryly that he was not used to such stationery and that if he had to sign anything it would need to be suitably prepared. A discussion arose, Hassanein came in, and finally it was agreed that the King would be allowed to retain his royal functions if he would immediately call Nahhas Pasha to form a new government. It was probably a good solution for Lampson too, for however powerful he may have been, surrounded with all the might of the British empire armed for war, it could hardly have been considered an act of good statesmanship to arouse the enmity of the whole country in the middle of wartime.

February 4, 1942, was to be an important date in contemporary events, since it was to demonstrate, for later armed groups, the quick way to attain power. Had the Wafd in 1942 rejected the British proposal and shown some sense of national solidarity with the Palace, it would perhaps have avoided having to submit to the same fate as the monarchy in 1952 and could have remained an interesting element within the country. But once the Wafd had acceded to the British demand, doubt was to arise in the minds of many as to the worth of this party—especially under its leadership at the time.

With one blow the British had succeeded in striking at the two principal institutions of the country: the credibility of the Wafd and the invulnerability of the monarchy. This was to be the culminating point of a British policy of 'divide and rule,' a strategy which was perfectly normal in politics, but which was to leave the nation with little possibility of any political cohesion.

The family was as divided in its passions as the rest of the country. There were the pro-Germans and the pro-British, for the already stated reasons, and there were those critical of the palace and those who were still being hoodwinked by the Wafd. In actual fact none of them mattered much, since they had all been reduced to official inactivity. All public careers were closed to this often energetic group of persons. When my brother Ismail wanted to join the army, the King refused his consent despite the fact that he was a close friend of his and boon companion. He finally made his way into the armed forces by volunteering in 1948 during the first Palestine war, in which circumstances he had to be accepted like any other citizen. He was a good pilot and had an active war record, but when hostilities ceased he was struck from the list of honors and decorations to which he was entitled. It was rumored, and there is absolutely no doubt about it, that the King was being deliberately isolated by his entourage and influenced against his paternal relatives. For already after King Fuad's death, a group of people had nicknamed the Muhammad Ali family 'La Famille du Défunt,' that is to say 'the deceased's family.' One must not overlook such trivialities, for they were symptomatic of a deeper crisis than just court intrigues. There was something prophetic in this mortuary appellation, something had come to an end, something was coming to an end.

Wealthy members of the family, such as Prince Youssouf Kemal or Prince Omar Toussoun and others, used their fortunes and energies to support intellectual, scientific, or artistic enterprises, and within the limits of private means to help the plight of the poor. It was revealed at Prince Omar Toussoun's death that he was helping three hundred villages that were in a particularly bad state, and two thousand needy families in Alexandria. He also kept in repair and himself supervised the desert wells vital to nomadic life. The desert was well known to him, as he was an archeologist who had made some interesting finds in those regions. All this goes perhaps to explain why he had the reputation of being rather tight-fisted with his immediate family!

At Prince Omar Toussoun's funeral in Alexandria, a crowd turned out to follow the coffin of the man who must have been in many cases their benefactor. He was buried in the center of the city at the Mosque of Nabi Daniel. The cemetery containing the remains of other members of the family, among them my grandfather, was destroyed in 1956, but after negotiations the bones of the deceased were allowed to be taken away and they were reburied in the cemetery of the Khedive Tewfik in Cairo. In Libya, Prince Omar Toussoun's memory is still cherished for having helped Libyan patriots over half a century ago, and a square has been named after him.

Prince Omar Toussoun's concern with welfare was part of Alexandria lore, but to the rest of the country his actions and those of other public-minded persons in the family passed virtually unknown. This was often due to their own discretion, but also to an unstable political climate. If anything was done on such a scale that it could not help being noticed, it was carefully ignored or else played down by government officials or the press. These persons nearly always had political affiliations, not necessarily leftist, but all thought they could benefit by undermining the established order and fish in troubled waters.

During King Farouk's minority, an atmosphere of sabotage was started by the Wafd. A move was made to curtail the King's constitutional powers, and a paramilitary force, the 'Blue Shirts,' eerily reminiscent of the Nazi 'Brown Shirts,' was created. After considerable difficulties, this military element independent of state institutions was disbanded, and the King's prerogatives were maintained by the Council of Regents.

Coming to the throne at a very young age at the beginning of a world conflict, finding himself immediately opposed by the Wafd, influenced into suspicion of his paternal family, publicly humiliated by the British, King Farouk's position was not an enviable one. His power seems to have stemmed from the prestige of his office, and his own immense popularity. No one who did not see the Egyptian people with their enormous generosity of heart acclaim their young prince can have an idea of what popularity is. I have seen crowds dance as he went by, and nothing that brainwashing or organized propaganda can produce will ever be as moving as this spontaneous demonstration of affection. His popularity spread beyond the frontiers of his country, and his portrait adorned both shops and homes in many Middle Eastern states. He was the hope of a whole generation.

But this was not to be. A clear and concise political history of his period, written by His Excellency Hassan Youssef Pasha, will hopefully be published. Some people still like to divide Farouk's reign into two parts: in the first, a handsome young king performing his task conscientiously;

and, in the second, a disillusioned man looking at the world through weary and cynical eyes. To his credit, one should remember that he was an unflinching patriot who by means of negotiations had moved the British out of the cities to a small region on the Suez Canal. This could probably also have been negotiated into a complete evacuation, as British rule in India was coming to an end. Of all the wars over Palestine, his in 1948 was the one in which our tiny army was to advance farthest into enemy territory, until it was stopped by a British and American embargo on importing ammunitions and arms. And, finally, it was during his reign that an attempt was made to unite the region politically by creating the Arab League—an effort that was quite successful until his departure from Egypt, at which point chaos broke loose over the Near East.

For those that like to fix a date for a change in King Farouk's behavior, they usually settle quite conveniently on the time of his car accident in 1943 at Qassasin. I prefer to think that an accumulation of events, starting with the palace incident of 1942, is more likely to have upset him. After this, there seems to have been a deterioration in his health and he began to put on weight. Of the change in his physical appearance he must have been painfully aware, as he once said to a foreigner: "Do you think it is amusing to be a king, fat, bald, and almost blind?" But there also seems to have been an incomprehensibly pessimistic streak in him that one could discern much earlier on when, at the height of his popularity, he coined the witty but autodestructive quip: "Soon there will only be five kings in the world, the four in a pack of cards and the King of England."

During this second part of his reign the most revolting slander began to be organized and spread against him by people sometimes so close to him that he refused to retaliate or have them silenced. Forces representing political or personal motives, and the most differing personal and political aims, joined together to plot his downfall— which they so successfully achieved. To quote Aunt Emina, who said quite simply: "He was greatly sinned against." However, many of his enemies are also buried in the ruins that they helped to create.

My personal contact with King Farouk was always of the pleasantest; I remember him courteous and good-natured. His smile had struck me that first time when we met at Montaza as children, and it did not waver or change with age. It had something eternal, like the smile on certain pharaonic statues.

When he died I was sincerely moved, and I was touched to see that I was not the only one. His body arrived by airplane from Italy at night, in a coffin covered with the old Egyptian green flag. He was not allowed to be buried in his tomb next to his father in the mosque of Rifai; he was placed instead in the same tomb as his great-grandfather, Ibrahim Pasha, in the old family cemetery near Imam al-Shafei. The burial took place in the night of his arrival, between two and five in the morning, in the solitary presence of his two sisters, Princesses Fawzia and Faika, and Princess Fawzia's husband. A week later permission was granted for twelve members of the family to attend a short ceremony, when we were allowed to say a prayer and listen to the recitation of the Quran beside his tomb. We were not allowed to bring flowers, but this annoyed me and I brought a wreath of red and blue blooms, the family colors, which I had laid in front of the tomb without any incident.

Princess Faika told me that when he was being buried, she made him a solemn pledge that she would have him reburied next to his father at Rifai. Many years later, through her saintly devotion, courage, and personal prestige, and after great difficulties had been surmounted, she succeeded in doing so. His son has built over his resting place a monument in white marble. It is not placed in the chamber which he should have occupied and which was offered for the demise of the last Shah of Iran, but stands in a passageway opposite the entrance to his father's tomb. There is something stark and surprising about this monument in white marble; it seems to stand somewhat apart in that otherwise colorful mosque.

One of the most striking features of King Farouk's period—and one that flourished more and more to the very end, whereas politics seemed to have fallen into a quagmire—was the work done by ladies of Egyptian society in social services. This should be a matter of pride to feminists all over the world, and a very sincere tribute should be paid to these ladies, who, under the leadership of members of the royal family, worked in many charitable organizations with unflagging energy and generosity. Not satisfied with organizing relief from Cairo, they would go in person to regions infested with epidemics and work in often uncomfortable conditions with rewarding results. My brother Ismail, too, participated personally, going to Upper Egypt and working with the peasants during the great malaria epidemic. Modern hospitals were created and were wonderfully well supervised; mobile dispensaries and canteens were organized.

Many of these institutions had started much earlier. In 1909 Princess Ayn al-Hayat, daughter of Prince Ahmed Rifaat and a favorite niece of the Khedive Ismail, started a dispensary at Abdeen financed by herself and other members of the family. This was the modest beginning of what was to become the 'Muhammad Ali Benevolent Society.' Princess Ayn al-Hayat stipulated that the president should always be a princess of the family, and that only women could be committee members—a highly advanced social event in the Near East, where most women were still secluded in harems.

This organization was to grow and flourish until literally millions were to benefit from it. I shall quote some statistics given by Aunt Emina, who herself worked actively in it: "By 1952 Cairo alone could boast two hospitals, three dispensaries, and eleven flying units with temporary quarters in the poorest parts of the city and suburbs. At the end of 1952 the annual total of persons treated at all branches had risen to 1,583,964."[1] Unfortunately, the hospitals of today, although still active, have fallen into some neglect in comparison with the vigilant administration of the abovementioned ladies.

These charitable institutions were to raise funds in many ways, but most spectacular were the annual balls given in aid of the Muhammad Ali Benevolent and the Red Crescent societies. They were great social events, splendidly organized, and brought in large amounts for these causes.

King Farouk's reign is associated in my mind with a sort of tidal wave of entertainment. Much of course was sparked off by the King's youthful energy, in which all his generation participated. But in the second part of his reign an unfortunate family life drove him farther and farther afield until he could also be seen at times in public places and clubs, a thing that was to leave him open to criticism. Within our own family, a round of parties got started with the visit of the Empress Fawzia (of Iran) to her homeland. Word was spread that entertainment should be provided for her, and a series of parties got under way. They were charming small gatherings,

---

[1] Emine Foat Tugay, *Three Centuries: Family Chronicles of Turkey and Egypt.* London: Oxford University Press, 1963.

and although not particularly amusing they were a pleasant enough manner in which to spend an evening.

The most numerous and talked-of parties were those given by Princess Chivekiar, who was the great hostess of the period. She was a delightful old lady with a quiet charm that worked equally well on young and old. How many times have I seen young people who were on duty visits at her house linger on much longer than was necessary! Originally her parties were not too large, and every Sunday there was a little soirée for the King and the family which we used to call 'Aunt Chivekiar's Sundays.' They were held in different parts of her palace, or with a different decor, to create a change of atmosphere. They were always pleasant in a quiet sort of way, and very small—I don't think there were ever more than twenty persons present. One might have said that they were really dinner parties with a little dancing afterward.

After a while, her receptions became bigger and bigger until all Cairo society was to be found there: Egyptian notables and their families; the diplomatic corps; during the war many Allied officers and crowned heads in exile; and, finally, anyone of mark passing through or residing in the country. Her two principal parties were held on New Year's Eve and on February 11, the King's birthday. When her palace, which was situated opposite the parliament buildings, overflowed with guests, a big marquee would be set up in the grounds. One would reach it by passing through what was normally a very handsome dining room of colored marble, from which a white marble staircase led to a lovely Turkish baroque garden, also of marble, with a white and gold kiosk and fountain, which, uprooted, can now be seen in a café in what remains of the Azbakiya Gardens. But in happier days, in Princess Chivekiar's palace, it preceded the main garden, which was reached by a few shallow steps and extended to Qasr al-Aini Street.

These complicated affairs started at half past nine (half an hour before the King's arrival) and would go on until morning, when footmen would pass among the remaining guests with trays of hot drinks—coffee, chocolate, or consommé. Credit for the organization of these occasions must go to the Princess's fifth husband, Ilhamy Hussein Pasha. He was a handsome person, and many a feminine heart fluttered at the sound of his name. He had the help of a colorful household staff, headed by a delightful English butler, Spencer, renowned for his polishing of silver, who was backed up by handsome young lackeys of different nationalities in eighteenth-century European costumes but wearing on their heads red tarbooshs with golden tassels—a rather baroque touch not to be seen in other households. The kalfas wore long Turkish robes of embroidered red velvet, whilst the berberine (Nubian) servants were in shalwar trousers, embroidered boleros, and stiff, starched white shirts and collars; on their heads they wore more normal tarbooshs with black tassels.

At random I conjure up family images: of Aunt Chivekiar in a large, spreading, complicated black-velvet dress with a splendid necklace of turquoises and diamonds; Aunt Béhidjé in the simplest of gowns over her stout figure, her round homely face with no visible makeup, but her twinkling eyes not missing a thing behind her spectacles; on her spare gray hair a flat diamond tiara and around her neck a necklace containing its famous pink diamond the size of an egg; Neslishah Sultane in white lace, radiant, imperial; the Empress Fawzia, very delicate, a multicolored jeweled butterfly in her black hair; the King, good-humored, a cigar in hand, moving from group to group; and Ilhamy Pasha courteously looking after everyone.

As the years went by, these parties became burdened with too many theatrical attractions and *tableaux vivants*, at least from the point of view of the younger set, and some would leave discreetly to go dancing in a less rarefied atmosphere. But I believe these shows were put on deliberately to amuse the King, who did not dance much and did not partake of alcoholic beverages.

I remember my first party on coming back from England was at Taher Pasha's. As the King did not drink, no alcohol was served, but since this might have proved a bit hard for some guests, a bar was set up in a discreet room, where one could have a quick drink. But when it was a big soirée, as at Princess Chivekiar's, the King waived this restraint and those who wanted to drink could do so even if he did not. He was a religious man who followed religious precepts strictly and thus set an example but did not impose it on others or ever make a show of it.

A couple of years after my return to Cairo, I was struck by the confusing, clashing situation of the country, where social jealousy and envy among those that should have known better and who had already obtained much was rife and destructive. And I remember saying to a cousin that I thought that we were on the verge of a revolution. Yet after a time I was to be among the foremost to be lulled into a sense of false security (perhaps grown-up life is like this, I thought). And when I overheard a foreigner at a large party say, "Egypt is a ripe fruit ready to be picked by the first person who raises his hand to take it," I had changed so much that I was quite indignant and attributed his words to envy of our prosperity in a world racked by war.

Yet more and more signs of unrest were clearly visible: violent demonstrations of university students, political assassinations (unfortunately of the most worthy people), a free press maligning surreptitiously, and then more and more openly, all forms of stability, and finally—most important of all—an unstable political situation with a continual change of government. There no longer seemed to be anyone at the helm. The best that could be said is that in general the country was prosperous, with a sound economy and no foreign debts, the frontiers safe. But one felt it was not doing much to better itself, and there seemed to be no radical plan to help the poor—even if this is a most complex and debatable problem. The Muhammad Ali Benevolent Society, the Red Crescent, and other charities were humanitarian institutions, not political solutions.

Overall, the situation was stagnant, if not bad. It is true that many of the rich were flaunting their wealth in a distasteful manner, but then the poor were allowed to fend for themselves, which some did very successfully, as many high officials and personalities were of the most modest background. There were no social barriers to people of talent, but only their personal economic handicaps at birth. It was an open society. Nothing could be more misleading than to represent the pashas as some sort of feudal caste. The title 'Pasha' was not hereditary but was bestowed on a person for personal merit or services rendered to the country, a bit like a knighthood or life-peerage, and would go to people in the most diverse walks of life. One might be a big industrialist from the Levant, an Egyptian general in either the army or the police, or a brilliant intellectual like Taha Hussein, who reached the rank of cabinet minister and won international fame. The son of a pasha inherited no title but was referred to by the courtesy title 'Bey,' a form of address that is still being bandied about quite freely today.

The government system was both democratic and sound, but perhaps at a critical moment there lacked a gifted person to take the country out of the political deadlock in which it found itself. And certainly foreign influences and interferences began to be talked about and felt.

Powerless and, as mentioned before, reduced to complete inactivity, the family could do nothing but fume with rage and quote pages from a more energetic past. But no one seemed to have a really constructive plan for the future. Parties and amusements became a little more tactful, but not much. Muhammad Taher Pasha, the King's first cousin, redoubled his good works among sporting circles; he also generously invited the Vienna Philharmonic, under Clemens Kraus, and the Berlin Philharmonic, under Wilhelm Furtwängler, to come to Cairo at his expense for a series of concerts. An apotheosis in private donations to charities occurred, but the most discerning members of foreign communities were beginning to leave the country.

An unpleasant feeling of unrest began to be felt everywhere. After a family luncheon at Abdeen, for example, in honor of the birth of Prince Ahmed Fuad, the King's son and heir, the car slowly wound its way in the square in front of the palace through a ragged crowd who pressed hostile faces to the window panes. It turned out to be a politically organized gathering, but that it should happen was significant.

Habits could not change overnight; people continued to order fresh salmon from the North Sea, and ladies to spend fortunes on Parisian novelties. Then on January 26, 1952, a beautiful cloudless day, the trumpets of doom sounded in an unmistakable manner. I was lunching with a friend at his home in Garden City when we noticed that the sky was turning from blue to a delicate gray. In the morning I had been advised not to go to town as there were some more tiresome demonstrations. But this was no tedious student affair. Cairo was burning, and the change of color we had noticed in the sky was the ashes of the burning city being gently wafted in our direction.

Alarm at last. We telephoned my brother Ismail, who was living in a bachelor's flat in town. He answered that he was all right but did not wish to talk too much, as the flat was filled with smoke from the burning building, which made him cough. He was sitting patiently in an armchair with a revolver at his side in case he needed to defend himself. The center of town was in the hands of carefully organized mobs who burned buildings and cars, but did not loot. All the same, a terrible massacre occurred at the English Turf Club with gruesome details, and loss of life was sustained elsewhere. A particularly tragic case was Shepheard's Hotel, which went up in a blaze while the previous night's shift of servants were fast asleep below stairs. Almost no one escaped the conflagration.

In other places the crowds would call up with characteristic bonhomie at the frightened citizenry peering from their windows: "Wait, wait until nightfall. We are going to get you tonight." Or shout advice about the best way to fall to a family crawling one by one on a ladder they were using to bridge the gap between their burning home and a neighboring building— while everyone roared with laughter. For hours the center of town was the prey of these sinister mobs. The police remained inactive; in all fairness they were probably not equipped for such a situation. But what was odd was that the army did not move in until four in the afternoon and finally restored order by nightfall. The government was Wafdist.

Fortunately neither the fire nor the mob reached Ismail, but when a week later I ventured into town I was appalled to see the city to which I was so attached in shambles, the gutted edifices, the abandoned scorched cars, rubble still to a certain extent strewn over sidewalks and streets, and I fled this almost incomprehensible vision of mutilation to nearby Lebanon.

When I came back after a fortnight, Cairo was still under martial law. Barricades stood at strategic points, and a curfew had been imposed at night, for which we had to have special passes to be able to move through the once-gay city, which now lay silent and still. It is generally agreed that those responsible for this tragic event were of different political affiliations and had joined forces with the tacit approval of certain people in high positions. The organization had been quite remarkable, as many of the buildings had been sprayed with inflammable matter the previous day and those who had noticed it had mistaken it for an insecticide.

Summertime came and I went to Alexandria with the intention of going to Europe for a holiday. The Italian ship on which I was supposed to leave was reputed to have a good cuisine and I had invited friends, including my dear cousins Princess Faiza and her husband, Muhammad Ali Raouf Bülent, to a farewell luncheon. But somehow everything seemed to go wrong and in the middle of the meal I was assailed by a terrible feeling of foreboding and disaster. I called the captain to tell him I would not leave, and asked him whether it was possible to have my luggage and car put ashore, and, if it was too late, whether he could have them brought back on his return journey. He was kindness itself and had everything set back on land while we moved to the Yacht Club to finish our luncheon, from which vantage point we watched the ship sail away two hours late, thanks to my irrational behavior! Bülent said I had made him so nervous that to dispel the tension we were to go later on to the races.

Bülent was one of the most hypersensitive and charming persons I have ever met. He could turn his attention successfully to almost any subject: archeology, gardening, cooking, interior decoration, organization in general, and in later years to mystic meditation and teaching. He had an abundance of *joie de vivre* and always saw the more humorous side of things without neglecting the serious. He too was a cousin, since he was the grandson of Princess Fatma, a daughter of the Khedive Ismail who played an important role in founding Cairo University.

Princess Fatma was quite pretty (she had the reputation of being a beauty) in a shortish and plump manner, with fine chestnut hair and tiny feet, but she was also known for being rather vain. She had an extraordinary passion for jewels, and it was fortunate that she was married to Prince Toussoun, who could provide her with whatever she wanted. The result was quite a staggering collection of personal jewelry, as can be seen in her portrait.

During the Khedive Abbas Hilmi's reign, a government delegation asked her for a donation to help found Cairo University. Like most of the Khedive Ismail's children, she considered herself in straitened circumstances and, instead of giving a sum of money, she gave her jewels, to which she added her house at Bulaq al-Dakrur, now the Agricultural Museum, and four hundred feddans of her best lands. The Khedive Abbas Hilmi, accompanied by his cabinet ministers, called on her to thank her for her generosity in the name of the nation. And in this manner Cairo University was founded. In her last years Princess Fatma accomplished the pilgrimage to the Holy Places and some time after this died.

As we see, Princess Faiza was Princess Fatma's niece, and Muhammad Ali Raouf Bülent, although older than his wife, was one generation further away in his relationship to her through his grandmother. This happened quite often, and my brother, sisters, and myself were much younger than our first cousins.

The season in Alexandria passed pleasantly, with a lot of swimming, dancing, and picknicking, usually in the same company that had been aboard ship. On the eve of July 23, Faiza and Bülent organized a fishing expedition in Alexandria harbor by lantern light. We fished all night in the warm balmy air without any very good results, and toward early morning we headed back to the wharf, where our cars were waiting. On the way we passed the royal yacht, the *Mahroussa*, which was working up steam. My second cousin Fayed Sabet, Ismet Hanem Effendi's younger son, who was there with us, pointed a finger at the funnel of the *Mahroussa* and—alluding to the unstable political situation—jokingly said, "I see there must have been another change of government." We all laughed, and heedlessly headed for home and sleep.

Next day we woke to find it had not been a cabinet reshuffle, but a military *coup d'état*. It was the beginning of the end of the monarchy in Egypt, and the start of the present-day regime. Three days later King Farouk abdicated in favor of his infant son, who was proclaimed king as Ahmed Fuad II. With the baby King and his closest family, the ex-King boarded the *Mahroussa* for exile, while a twenty-one gun salute was fired, no longer in his honor, but for the little royal infant. A huge silent crowd filled the square in front of the Ras al-Tin Palace to watch the departure of the royal party from the pier of the palace, whose white walls and windows were gently reflected in the calm sea.

The Princesses Fawzia and Faiza, wanting to bid farewell to their brother the King, had to ask permission from the new authorities. Their request was granted, and two government cars were sent. The Princesses and their husbands rode in the second car, which was preceded by a car containing officials to accompany them to the palace. After the King had departed, the Princesses rode back once more in the second car, but the first was no longer there. Princess Fawzia was seated in the back, next to the right-hand window; her husband, Ismail Shirine Bey, sat next to her, and Princess Faiza on the other side. Bülent was in front, next to the driver.

Without any escorts, the car had difficulty moving through the dense and now restless crowd, and at one point a little urchin climbed on the roof of the Princesses' car and started beating on it as if it were a musical instrument. Princess Faiza, with the extraordinary calm and composure that never left her, a truly royal trait, leaned her head out of the window and said to the child: "Be careful. You could fall down and hurt yourself!

It would be better for you to come down from up there." At this vision of sweetness and loveliness, the child smiled back at her and clambered down. After that the car proceeded without any further incidents.

One year later the monarchy was abolished, and all the possessions of the Muhammad Ali family were decreed confiscated, a decree that was to touch even our most distant relatives. My mother returned to her native land, and my sister Aicha went to Turkey to be with her Turkish daughter Nevin. The rest of us stayed on to watch the passing of an era and to follow Egypt's future.

Epilogue

If, by any chance, someone swept away by my enthusiastic description of the region of al-Marg should have the curiosity to visit the place, I must dissuade them from doing so. First, to reach it, you have to pass through a series of modern slums that overshadow some of the pleasanter buildings of a previous era. From there, after crossing the railway lines to where the Blunt domain used to be, with its handsome groves of mango trees, nothing remains; this is no more than a shabby suburb of other suburbs. On reaching the forest of Marg, you will find that the trees are sickly, and that there are many dead stumps pointing skyward because the irrigation channels have been filled in so as to grow some minor crop in their place.

Uncle Ala'adin's poplar trees, which had prospered well and were a lovely sight shimmering in the landscape, were torn down at about a meter from the ground and their jagged remains looked like some tragic Goya etching. Fortunately, an enterprising person finally uprooted them, putting them out of their misery. The great eucalyptus trees of Aunt Nimet's Marg, farther on, were the first to go; they were too great a temptation.

As for Shubra, there is now a handsome corniche that follows the Nile and leads there. The grounds of the old palace are filled with modern buildings, which are part of the University of Ain Shams.

Aunt Iffet's delightful little house stands derelict and boarded up, but some trees still surround it. Of course all the more ornamental vegetation on the platforms leading up to the house has gone, as have the marble urns, and it is difficult to imagine that this had once been a place of some charm and elegance.

The great marble quadrangle now belongs to the Faculty of Agriculture of Ain Shams University and can be visited by arrangement.

About Cairo itself, what shall I say? My feelings are too mixed up about it. Once you belong to a place, you are tied to it for better of for worse. So finally, to clear up my thoughts, I decided to ask a newly arrived friend for her impression of the city. And, bless her, she came out with a most comforting answer. Without hesitation she said, "It has tremendous dignity." Which I suppose has something to do with the great architectural monuments to be found there, and the spirit of its people.

Appendix

Family Trees

The Rulers

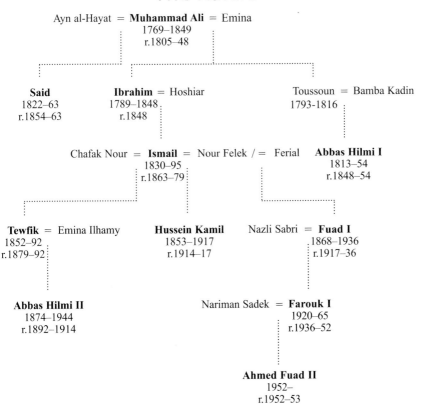

Ayn al-Hayat = **Muhammad Ali** = Emina
1769–1849
r.1805–48

Said
1822–63
r.1854–63

Ibrahim = Hoshiar
1789–1848
r.1848

Toussoun = Bamba Kadin
1793-1816

Chafak Nour = **Ismail** = Nour Felek / = Ferial
1830–95
r.1863–79

Abbas Hilmi I
1813–54
r.1848–54

Tewfik = Emina Ilhamy
1852–92
r.1879–92

Hussein Kamil
1853–1917
r.1914–17

Nazli Sabri = **Fuad I**
1868–1936
r.1917–36

Abbas Hilmi II
1874–1944
r.1892–1914

Nariman Sadek = **Farouk I**
1920–65
r.1936–52

Ahmed Fuad II
1952–
r.1952–53

The Author's Immediate Family

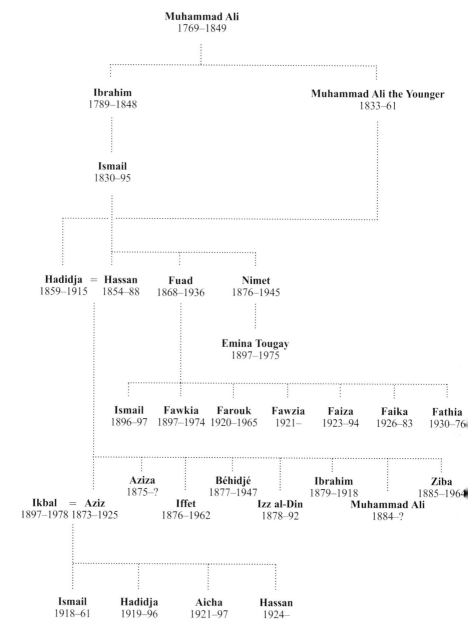

Muhammad Ali
1769–1849

Ibrahim
1789–1848

Muhammad Ali the Younger
1833–61

Ismail
1830–95

Hadidja = **Hassan**
1859–1915 1854–88

Fuad
1868–1936

Nimet
1876–1945

Emina Tougay
1897–1975

Ismail **Fawkia** **Farouk** **Fawzia** **Faiza** **Faika** **Fathia**
1896–97 1897–1974 1920–1965 1921– 1923–94 1926–83 1930–76

Aziza
1875–?

Béhidjé
1877–1947

Ibrahim
1879–1918

Ziba
1885–1964

Ikbal = **Aziz**
1897–1978 1873–1925

Iffet
1876–1962

Izz al-Din
1878–92

Muhammad Ali
1884–?

Ismail **Hadidja** **Aicha** **Hassan**
1918–61 1919–96 1921–97 1924–

138

Rulers' Wives and Children

Muhammad Ali

Emina of Nosratli	Tevhida, Ibrahim, Toussoun, Ismail, Hadidja
Madouran	No children
Ayn al-Hayat	Said Pacha
Montaz	Hassan
Mahivech	Ali Sadik Bey
Namchaz	Muhammad Abdel Halim
Ziba Hadidja	Muhammad Ali the younger
Chams Safa	Fatma al-Ruhiya
Shama Nour	Zeineb

Ibrahim Pacha

Hadidja (Birinci Kadin)	Muhammad Bey
Chivekiar	Ahmed Rifa'at
Hoshiar	Khedive Ismail
Ülfet	Moustafa Bahgat Ali Fazil
Kalzar	No children
Sa'aret	No children

Abbas I (son of Toussoun and Bambakadin)

Mahivech	Ibrahim Ilhamy
Chazdil	Moustafa, Princess Hawa
Hawaya	Muhammad Sadik, Aicha Sadika
Hamdam	No children
Perlanet	No children

Said Pacha

Indji	No children
Melekher	Muhammad Toussoun, Mahmoud

Ismail Pacha

Shehret	Tevhida, Fatma
Djananiar	Ibrahim Hilmi, Zeineb
Djechme Affet	No children, adopted a Circassian girl
Chafak Nour	Muhammad Tewfik
Nour Felek	Hussein Kamel
Misl Melek	Hassan
Djehan Shah	Mahmoud Hamdi
Hour Djehan	Emina
Ferial	Fuad
Misl Djehan	Djemila
Felek Naz	Reshid Bey
Gamal Nour	Ali Djemal
Neshedil	Emina, Nimet
Bizim Alem	No children

Muhammad Tewfik

Emina Ilhamy	Abbas Hilmi II, Muhammad Ali Tewfik, Nazli, Hadidja, Nimetallah

Abbas II

Ikbal	Abd al-Moneim, Muhammad Abd al-Qadir, Emina, Attiatallah, Fathiya, Chevket
Gevidan	No children

Hussein Kamel

Ayn al-Hayat	Kemaleddin, Kazime, Ahmed Nazim
Melek	Kadria, Semiha

Ahmed Fuad I

(when Prince)

Chivekiar	Ismail, Fawkia

(later when King)

Nazli	Farouk, Fawzia, Faiza, Faika, Fathia

Farouk I

Farida (Safinaz Zulficar)	Ferial, Fawzia, Fadia
Nariman Sadek	Ahmed Fuad II

(Ahmed Fuad II married and divorced Fadila)

Index